The Value Killers

Nuno Fernandes

The Value Killers

How Mergers and Acquisitions Cost Companies Billions—And How to Prevent It

palgrave
macmillan

Nuno Fernandes
Lisbon, Portugal

ISBN 978-3-030-12215-7   ISBN 978-3-030-12216-4   (eBook)
https://doi.org/10.1007/978-3-030-12216-4

Library of Congress Control Number: 2019931026

Cover Design by eStudio Calamar
Original concept by Kyryl Lakishyk

This Palgrave Macmillan imprint is published by the registered company Springer Nature Switzerland AG.
The registered company address is: Gewerbestrasse 11, 6330 Cham, Switzerland

To Isabel, Francisco, and Luísa

Acknowledgments

This book has been developed with the support of numerous individuals. I have greatly benefited from my regular interactions with hundreds of executives from all backgrounds, including CEOs, CFOs, and other senior executives of many companies around the world, teaching sessions, developing company-specific programs, as an adviser in consulting projects, or simply informal conversations. I am grateful to them for sharing their wisdom with me and inspiring many of the ideas in the book.

Many business professionals were kind enough to read various chapters and share their observations with me. Among this group, a special word of thanks goes to all the executives who were super-generous with their time, through several rounds of interviews. They have helped me in many different ways, to understand better the details of some deals, the complexity and challenges of day-to-day running of successful M&As, and overall, generously shared their knowledge with me. These were the executives interviewed in this book:

- Anastasia Kovaleva
- Casper Kirketerp-Moeller
- Halbart Völker
- Harish Krishnaswamy
- Huibert Vigeveno
- Jordi Costa
- Karim Karoui
- Ken Sasaki
- Liana Logiurato
- Luciano Poli
- Marcus Hanana

- Michael Jeppesen
- Naveed Pathan
- Sandeep Jalan
- Stefan Wanjek
- Stefan Koch

My thinking has been shaped by my work over the past years with all my students and co-authors. They helped me refine the ideas in this book through their finance classes at IMD, in MBA and executive education courses, and in many companies around the world. Over the years, they provided additional thoughts and insights that helped shape the book that you now hold in your hands. Moreover, I have had a number of co-authors in different case studies that deserve a special mention here, as many of the ideas here came out of joint work we did in the past.

I am also extremely grateful to my colleagues at IMD, namely, the team of editors Susan Broomfield, Beverley Lennox, Lindsay McTeague, Michelle Perrinjaquet, and Susan Stehli. Then there has been my editor at Palgrave, Tula Weis, who has been consistently encouraging, directing, and pushing my work forward. I also appreciate the support received from a very good colleague and friend, Kyryl Lakishyk, who used his outstanding creativity skills to create the design of the cover of this book. I am also deeply indebted to my assistants Walter Giardello, and Fátima Silva, who supported several production and editing tasks of this book.

This book could not have been written without the love and support of my family. My wife, Isabel, has read and commented on different drafts of this book and has always been a sounding board and source of ideas for my work. And my two children helped me with their patience and uncomplainingly sacrificed time with their dad on account of my work on this book.

Contents

Introduction

On August 18, 2011, U.S. computer maker Hewlett-Packard (HP) announced the acquisition of British software maker Autonomy for $11.1 billion. The deal was positioned as part of HP's new "strategic" direction toward the higher-growth software sector and away from the declining PC business.

The announcement followed months of accelerated due diligence and negotiations by an internal HP team supported by two different investment banks. At the end of the process, HP's board of directors voted unanimously to approve a final offer of £25.50 ($41.82) per share of Autonomy—a 64 percent premium above the previous day's closing share price of £15.58.[1]

The reaction by investors was swift and negative. HP's share price fell 25 percent in the two days after the announcement, and it kept tumbling amid criticisms from market analysts (and some shareholders) that HP had grossly overpaid.

A month later, HP announced that CEO Léo Apothecker was stepping down.

Then, on November 20, 2012, HP issued some stunning news: it was writing off $8.8 billion of the original $11.1 billion investment and accusing Autonomy officials of accounting improprieties and misrepresentations. (Note that *none* of the 15 financial, legal, and accounting firms hired by both companies raised a red flag before the closing.[2]) Shortly thereafter, HP's chairman and its longest-serving directors resigned from the company.

*   *   *

Although the HP-Autonomy acquisition is an extreme example of a failed, value-destroying transaction, the case is far from unique. Between 1980 and 2001, mergers and acquisitions (M&As) by large companies destroyed $226 billion in shareholder wealth.[3]

Regardless, a growing number of chief executives will continue pursuing growth through M&As, and most of these deals will continue to fail and/or destroy shareholder value.

As of this writing, there is speculation that the business world is on the *verge* of a new "merger wave" following a record-breaking year for M&As. In 2016, $4.9 trillion in global transactions were announced, breaking the 2007 record for total deal value.[4] Although organic growth remains important, a 2016 EY survey found that a "near-record" 57 percent of companies planned to actively pursue acquisitions in the coming 12 months.

Of course, executives have long pursued inorganic growth strategies to quickly boost corporate performance and acquire new product lines, business models, technologies, and so on. Hence, the motivations behind the latest round of deal-making are nothing new.

What *is* new is the sheer scope and intensity of disruptive forces facing many companies and industries. Fueled by the digitalization of the global economy, changes in the competitive environment require that organizations innovate at a faster and faster pace to ensure their very survival. Unparalleled technological advances, disruptive new business models, the blurring of sector lines, and fast-changing consumer expectations are prompting many firms to rethink their strategies and reinvent themselves at lightning speed.

Speed has always been a key advantage of M&As compared to organic growth, but in an era when, for example, IT companies keep emerging from seemingly nowhere to successfully compete in industries from automobile manufacturing and financial services to television production, transportation and mobility, and hospitality, established players have a compelling incentive to quickly buy their way back toward competitive advantage. Organically building (and rebuilding) a strong competitive position takes time, but time is something in short supply in an environment that moves at the speed of computer servers. When time is of the essence, so is the need to boost growth velocity by rapidly acquiring the products and services, business models, and expertise that will ensure that the organization stays competitive and satisfies key stakeholders.

The Enduring Allure of 2 + 2 = 5

These trends, along with an improving global economy and cash-laden corporate balance sheets, are propelling the latest merger wave. However, even if this "wave" is a short-lived anomaly, mergers and acquisitions will continue playing an important role in companies' growth and expansion efforts. Merger waves occur in response to innovations and technological shocks across different industries, but the desire of chief executives to capture new cost and revenue synergies (to activate the alchemical 2 + 2 = 5 formula) will always be a tempting proposition.

There are several good reasons for organizations to buy instead of build. They include:

- *Speed.* The ability to achieve strategic goals (and size) faster than through organic growth.
- *Access to new capabilities. Technologies, processes, business models, intellectual property (IP), and other resources* (including human resources).
- *Increased product range.* Combining two companies can improve the end offer to consumers, giving the merged entity a stronger product portfolio from which it can generate considerable gains.
- *Greater distribution range.* Combining two companies can enlarge the distribution range and geographical scope of activities, allowing the cross-selling of products and services.
- *Increased manufacturing capabilities.* This happens when the target company has a technological edge that can be better leveraged as part of a combined and bigger organization.
- *Reduced operating and production costs.* Often, deals are justified by the creation of cost synergies whereby the final costs of goods or services can be reduced if the two firms merge.
- *Greater pricing power.* Deals can also be justified based on improvements in the competitive positioning if they lead to better pricing power.

Most Mergers Destroy Value

Over the decades, however, multiple studies have shown that most mergers and acquisitions fail to generate the anticipated synergies—and many actually destroy value instead of creating it. In other words, a significant percentage of M&As cause 2 + 2 to equal 3 instead of 5.

The percentage of transactions that result in failure or even value destruction varies, depending on the study, when it was conducted, the definitions used, and a host of other variables, but one commonly cited estimate is that 70–90 percent of deals fail,[5] which means they lead to value destruction from the (acquiring) shareholders' point of view.

If these statistics are a surprise, then your reaction is atypical. During my extensive consulting and teaching careers, I've encountered very few senior managers who were *not* aware that mergers and acquisitions are subject to high failure rates. In fact, whenever I cite figures like those above, the typical executive's response is: "I know, I know…" as opposed to "I don't believe it." The vast majority of executives are well aware of these statistics, even as many continue to make the same mistakes as their predecessors. Most are also aware of at least *some* of the major reasons for the disconcerting failure rate, but will nonetheless pursue bad deals, thinking (perhaps) that the daunting statistics apply to others, but not themselves.

The Usual Suspects

After the fact, many of those responsible for the deals that go bad will attribute the failures to cultural mismatches, problematic integrations, or both.

Make no mistake: culture and integration management are vital to the success of M&As and should never be neglected. At the same time, they are too often used as convenient "post-game" scapegoats by executives hoping to deflect blame from their own lack of insight, foresight, and preparation.

Obviously, no executive *consciously* pursues a value-destroying acquisition. That being said, the vast majority of bad deals can be traced to managers who practice faulty reasoning—faulty reasoning stemming from:

Ego and Emotion The CEO wishing to enhance his reputation as a Captain of Industry by getting his name in *The Financial Times* is far more likely to undertake deals for personal reasons instead of those in which potential synergies exist.

Empire Building This correlates with ego and emotion in that most empire builders "feel" that a bigger company is a better company.

Lack of Appropriate Board Oversight Too often, boards of directors are presented with final deals without receiving enough advance notice to prepare the right questions.

Overconfidence Recent studies of the behavior of CEOs and boards of directors reveal that a subset of these individuals are overconfident about their ability to identify good deals, thanks largely to their past successes in this arena. Because these individuals attribute past successes to *only* their own abilities, while attributing failures to external causes (a.k.a., "self-attribution bias"), they "tend to acquire other firms in subsequent (high-order) deals that trigger significantly lower returns to shareholders than the first deals." In some instances, this "leads them to initiate and carry out deals that destroy shareholder wealth."[6]

The "We Need to Do Something" Syndrome Unfavorable deals are more likely to be pursued when a company is flush with cash, and the leadership wants to do "something" (anything!) to boost growth, improve margins, "bury the competition," and so on, but has no idea whatsoever. Instead of carefully considering new goals and next steps, management pours the company's cash into a deal for which there's no economic rationale in order to satisfy the urge to do something "bold" and "proactive."

Greed In some cases, senior managers undertake deals to increase the size of their remuneration packages. It should be noted, however, that CEOs who hope to double their compensation by doubling the size of their companies will likely be disappointed. If a company doubles its size because of an M&A, the average increase in CEO compensation is 60 percent.[7]

Encouragement from Investment Banks The incentives for the investment banks involved in mergers and acquisitions are not always fully aligned with those of the buyers. Investment banks are paid upon completion of the deals, and their fees are directly proportional to deal size. Even if the deal destroys value for the acquiring company, the investment bank still earns a handsome fee. To put it kindly, the banks have been given a perverse incentive. The desire to generate a big fee could prompt a bank to encourage a deal that's not in the buyer's best interest.

"Strategic Acquisitions" When a rational analysis of the benefits of the merger cannot justify the premium to be paid for the target, the proponents of such deals sometimes turn to a phrase that's become clichéd from overuse. They argue that "this deal is strategic for us. We'd be crazy not to do it." Some managers seem to believe that once a deal is called "strategic," it will create value for the shareholders. Obviously, this is not the case at all, and shareholders may refuse to buy into an argument based on emotion rather than reason.

Diversification It's not the job of management to diversify the portfolios of the company's shareholders by acquiring companies in different sectors or with different product/service lines. Shareholders are capable of doing this themselves by buying the stock of other companies. (And historically, building a conglomerate is more likely to destroy value than create it.)

Collectively, these challenges (and others) tend to contribute to the *No. 1 reason* for M&A failure: **paying too high a premium for the target.** If the acquirer overpays, it's unlikely that the anticipated value will be created, even if all the expected synergies are realized on schedule.

The Road to Hell ...

If "the road to hell is paved with good intentions," so is the road to value-destroying mergers and acquisitions. After all, even executives who pursue the wrong deals for the wrong reasons are usually motivated by a desire to improve the company's financial health.

Unfortunately, even deals undertaken with good intentions—and for good reasons—are frequently derailed by any number of issues. The most common include poor preparation and planning, overestimating the potential synergies, and underestimating the amount of due diligence needed. Often, management also fails to consider (or it underestimates) the challenges posed by integrating the two entities, smoothing over culture clashes, and minimizing employee attrition (before, during, and after the closing of the deal).

One of the most common—and important—causes of M&A derailment is senior management's failure to hold anyone accountable for achieving the anticipated synergies. More often than not, this occurs when those leading transition teams are not the same people who are later charged with overseeing the newly acquired business units. Although synergies are identified and valuations calculated based on those synergies, no single manager's feet are later held to the fire to ensure that those synergies are achieved within the requisite timeframe.

Another common error made by buyers is moving too slowly through the M&A process. Because this can extend the bidding period, competitors may decide to poach employees and customers, or even make tempting acquisition offers of their own.

During the deal phase, it's also not unusual for an acquiring company to lose focus regarding the "mundane tasks" of actually running the business—of serving existing customers and acquiring new ones. Add to this poor or inadequate communications about the reasons for the deal, as well as what customers, employees, and other stakeholders should expect during and after the transition, and the deal could cause more problems than it solves. When it comes to retaining good employees, customers, and investors, uncertainty is not your friend.

The Five Golden Rules

What can be done to reverse this sad state of affairs? How can companies dramatically increase the odds that their future M&As will be among the minority that actually succeed? After all, even in the best of circumstances, M&As are exceedingly complex, making them difficult to successfully execute and manage. Do the challenges described above lend themselves to simple, elegant solutions?

Yes.

However, do *not* confuse phrases such as *elegant and simple* with those such as *fast and easy*. As a template for M&A success, the Five Golden Rules are conceptually simple, but neither fast nor easy to implement without rigorous planning and adept management of the deal's many moving parts.

Golden Rule 1: Don't Rely on Investment Bankers for Valuation Investment banks are good for roadshows and financing (and are sometimes required by regulators), but they should never be used for valuing or negotiating the deal. Because investment banks receive much larger fees when the deals are closed, bankers are always on the side of the deal, not the company's side.

Golden Rule 2: Avoid "Strategic" Deals In theory, there's nothing wrong with characterizing an acquisition as "strategic." In practice, though, the word is often misused by the champions of flawed deals to mask the shortcomings, silence a deal's opponents, or both. The "strategic" argument can be difficult to refute, which may be why some CEOs like to use it. Unfortunately, it is too often used when the numbers do not work but top managers still want to close the deal.

Golden Rule 3: Link the Before and After Companies must have a continuous process that links the pre-deal phase with the transaction period and the post-deal phase. The firms most likely to destroy value are those that fail to assign detailed responsibilities and strict accountability to the teams in charge of researching, planning, negotiating, and implementing the acquisition.

Golden Rule 4: Think Like a Financial Investor Executives must be ready to say no to deals that exceed the "walk-away price." They should not enter into auctions and should never fall in love with the deals. In addition, CEOs and boards must avoid making decisions based on overconfidence. This behavior can easily lead to value destruction. (In some respects, the CEO who relies on the "this deal is strategic" rationale is not unlike the president or prime minister who cites "national security concerns" to steamroll the opposition into ratifying his actions.)

Golden Rule 5: Move Fast and Communicate Transparently Companies that communicate quickly, constantly, and openly during M&As are better able to retain their focus and reduce uncertainty among customers and employees, especially the best employees of the target company. Because talent exodus is a big risk during most M&As, senior managers must be ready to answer the "What happens to me?" question before employees even ask it.

*   *   *

As we shall see, the fact that most M&As fail to create value for shareholders of the acquiring company is neither a random occurrence nor "bad luck," but the result of ignoring the five rules outlined above. These rules, which are based on extensive research (including case studies and executive interviews), are designed to maximize the odds of M&A success by providing executives with a template for distinguishing between deals that offer long-term growth opportunities and those likely to generate value-destroying activities.

If more companies follow the Five Golden Rules, then the coming years will witness an upsurge in not just the quantity of transactions but the quality as well.

Notes

1. Michael H. Moffett, Andrew Inkpen, and Lena Booth, "HP's Acquisition of Autonomy." Thunderbird School of Global Management, 2013.
2. Nadia Damouni and Nicola Leske, "In HP-Autonomy debacle, many advisers but little good advice." *Reuters*, November 21, 2012.
3. Sara B. Moeller, Frederik P. Schlingemann, and René M. Stulz, "Wealth destruction on a massive scale: A study of acquiring firm returns in the merger wave of the late 1990s," *Journal of Finance*.
4. "U.S. executives on M&A: full speed ahead in 2016," KPMG and Fortune Knowledge Group.
5. Clayton M. Christensen, Richard Alton, Curtis Rising, and Andrew Waldeck, "The Big Idea: The New M&A Playbook." *Harvard Business Review*, March 2011.
6. Kind, Axel and Twardawski, Torsten. "Board Overconfidence in Mergers & Acquisitions: A Self-Attribution Bias."
7. Nuno Fernandes, with M. Ferreira, P. Matos and K. Murphy, "Are US CEOs Paid More? New International Evidence." *The Review of Financial Studies*, Vol. 26 (2), February 2013.

1

Don't Rely on Investment Banks for Valuation

Like the Trojan horse of Homer's *Iliad*, HP's acquisition of Autonomy was the "gift" that kept on giving negative consequences.

To start, HP's stock price fell 25 percent in the two days following the announcement on August 18, 2011. Though it was difficult to pinpoint *all* the causes of this drastic decline, the general message was clear: the market did not believe that HP's direction was a promising one.

Then, as Autonomy's results faltered in the two quarters after the deal, HP took a harder look at its operating results and, in the spring of 2012, began raising serious questions about the financial records and revenue recognition practices of Autonomy. On November 20, 2012, HP announced that it was writing off $8.8 billion of its original $11 billion investment.

Normally, this would have been the end of the story as far as the press and public were concerned. But the deal made the headlines again when HP filed a lawsuit in the U.K., accusing former Autonomy CEO Mike Lynch and former CFO Sushovan Hussain of engaging in "improper transactions and accounting practices that artificially inflated and accelerated Autonomy's reported revenues," which had the effect of making Autonomy appear more profitable and growing faster than it actually was. Specifically, HP alleged (among other things) that Autonomy engaged in numerous "contrived transactions" that were devised to book revenue improperly. In some cases, HP said, Autonomy used third parties known as value-added resellers (VARs) to "fabricate or accelerate" sales that were reported as revenue.[1]

© The Author(s) 2019
N. Fernandes, *The Value Killers*, https://doi.org/10.1007/978-3-030-12216-4_1

Where Were the External Advisers?

Even if the charges are without merit, the fact that they *appear* to be credible begs the question: Why did none of the external advisers raise any red flags about these issues? For a transaction of this size, companies usually rely on a variety of advisers—from accounting firms and auditors to law firms and investment banks—to perform the due diligence, to provide strategic guidance, legal advice, and financing, and, most important, to uncover potential fraud and any legal and environmental liabilities. This deal was no exception to the rule. Between them, HP and Autonomy retained the services of 15 "brand name" institutions.[2]

Among HPs external advisers was the accounting firm Deloitte, which was tasked with vetting Autonomy's financials. (The company subsequently retained KPMG to audit Deloitte.) In addition, HP hired the boutique investment bank Perella Weinberg Partners to serve as lead adviser, along with Barclays. Banking advisers on both sides of the deal were paid a total of $68.8 million. On Autonomy's side was Qatalyst Partners, which specializes in tech deals and earned $11.6 million. Autonomy's investment bankers included UBS, Goldman Sachs, Citigroup, JPMorgan Chase, and Bank of America, which were each paid $5.4 million.[3]

Ultimately, HP management was responsible for the deal's failure. It wasn't the first time (nor will it be the last time) that an M&A fiasco could be traced to poor decision-making by corporate leaders. But as *Forbes* pointed out in a November 2012 analysis, the external advisers also deserve some of the blame for having *not* unearthed the negative information during due diligence. And this last failure highlights a fundamental flaw in the M&A process: investment banks (and sometimes other advisers) have a perverse incentive to ensure that each and every transaction is completed, and they have few tangible incentives to slow down or kill a deal.

To quote the *Forbes* post-mortem, "Most [advisers] are paid by the hour or through a success fee, giving them a monetary incentive to originate and consummate mergers and acquisitions.... [N]o single adviser wants to be seen as the one putting up roadblocks. Once a corporate client decides to go ahead with a transaction, its advisers are basically there to fulfill its wishes, not to question the wisdom of the decision. As momentum for the deal snowballs, and pressure to finalize it under tight deadlines builds, it is very difficult for any adviser to put a stop to it."[4]

Casper Kirketerp-Moeller, CEO of Clever A/S, noted that because investment banks are ranked and rated based on past successes, it's important for them that deals go through. "There's a great deal of pressure to conclude deals or find ways to conclude them."

Winners and Losers

Regardless of the merits of a particular M&A, investment bankers and CEOs are almost always happy when the deal closes. It is the *buyer's shareholders* who bear the burden if the deal turns out to be a lemon. So the usual winners are the investment banks, the lawyers, the accountants, the auditors, and the seller (otherwise, it would not close the deal), as well as the CEOs of both companies (including the target, as she/he usually receives a very nice check). The losers, again, are the buyer's shareholders—and it's *these losses* that I'm referencing when I say that, on average, mergers destroy value.

This is not to suggest that investment banks aren't key stakeholders in many M&A deals. They are. What they are *not*, however, is key *risk-takers after the transaction closes*. Mergers and acquisitions represent one of the most important sources of fee-based income for investment banks, and banks typically risk most of their income by agreeing to work on a contingency basis (for the "success fee"). The average success fee ranges from 1 to 3 percent of the deal value, and even at these apparently small percentages, the payouts for successful closings can be enormous. For example, the fees earned by the three investment banks that participated in Royal Dutch Shell's $70 billion takeover of British energy firm BG were estimated at $182.6 million. But that figure pales in comparison to the largest-ever fee that banks have earned from an M&A transaction. That "honor" belongs to the banks involved in the 1999 Vodafone acquisition of Mannesmann AG, who collected a staggering $530.7 million in combined fees.

The downside of the "success fee" is that a bank's considerable investment of time, money, and human resources will generate next to nothing if the transaction isn't finalized. Therefore, it's in the bank's interest to ensure that every deal *does* close. Bankers *do* risk tarnishing their reputations if they close too many failed deals or appear to have pushed clients into making unwise decisions, but as long as most deals don't rise to the level of the HP-Autonomy disaster, the reputation of an established bank will usually survive the negative publicity.

Speaking of reputation, one of the most important factors that helps banks secure future business is their ranking in the league tables. Here, the world's biggest banks are ranked for M&A advisory work based on the value of the deals in which they've been involved, as an adviser of either the target or the acquirer. A bank's position in the league tables is considered a measure of their experience and reputation. (For individual bankers, compensation is usually tied to the fees they help generate, as well as the number/quality of the relationships they cultivate.) Investment banks use league tables to promote themselves, but note that the tables highlight the monetary values of the completed deals—not the value creation produced by those deals!

Although investment banks are a necessary part of transactions, companies should not solely rely on them to provide a final valuation and to negotiate the deal, thanks to the inherent conflict of interest stemming from their fee structure.

Most M&As are driven by international investment banks that are not going to be engaged in the operational realities of the deal or become responsible for the implementation or achievement of the promised synergies. Managers who simply outsource the valuation to an investment bank may be risking their company's money and jeopardizing potential opportunities for significant value creation for their shareholders.

This does not mean that companies should not hire investment banks. On the contrary, M&A participants *must* use them in most cases that involve publicly traded companies. But management should always be sure to also seek advice from additional—and more objective—experts to mitigate the banks' conflict of interest.

Moreover, CEOs, CFOs, and other top executives need to be involved at the earliest possible stage of any merger and should understand how valuations are made, so they can maximize value creation for shareholders and steer their organizations toward identifying and assessing opportunities and risks.

Alternatives to the Success Fee

"Our industry is one in which the services of the leading investment bankers are all pretty much the same. So … reputation is what matters," said former Goldman Sachs Chairman John Whitehead. At the end of the day, investment bankers are people—people whose business is maximizing profits from the sale of their services—and advising *against* deals is a poor way to maximize profits. That said, most bankers *do* adhere to a set of ethical standards and are keen to enhance and maintain their personal reputations and those of the banks. For those reasons, said most of the executives and former bankers interviewed for this book, while some *individual* bankers are *always on the side of the deal,* most bankers look out for their clients' interests (up to a point). "Individuals differ within banks: there are the people who really care about, and develop, a relationship with a selling and a buying company, and there are people purely driven by fees. And those people are known," said Anastasia Kovaleva, a consultant with Bain & Company (and a former investment banker), who has worked on numerous deals.

Liana Logiurato, Global Head of M&A for Syngenta International, agreed. "My simple view is that it all comes down to individuals – their personal ethics and whether they want to act in the best interest of their clients."

Given the perverse incentive built into the success fee, you might think that acquiring companies (especially) would be eager to embrace the alternatives—hourly rates, higher retainer fees, or some combination of higher retainers and lower success fees. (*Note:* Retainers are typically non-refundable, paid in milestone-based installments or as an upfront lump sum, and are not contingent on the deal's outcome.) But, said many of the experts interviewed, you would be mistaken if you thought so.

The vast majority of companies balk at the idea of raising the retainer or having bankers work for hourly rates. Why? Because lowering the success fee (which is a *contingency* fee) would transfer certain risks from the bank to the buyer and seller. In short, most acquirers and targets don't want to pay hefty upfront fees for deals that may never close.

Halbart Völker, Managing Director and Head of Industries Corporate Banking for NIBC Bank NV, neatly summarized this attitude,

> [T]he argument we always get from the client is that they do not want to have a huge cost upfront, particularly in case the deal doesn't go through. So it's usually the client that skews much more towards the success-based fee, and therefore automatically accepts the inherent issues that come with that. I would say 99 out of 100 clients … do not want to have huge expenses if the deal doesn't go through. And if the deal goes through, then [they pay] only a percentage of the deal's cost, which is anything up to (say) five percent.… But if you have to explain to shareholders that you incurred an upfront cost to avoid a bad deal, that's still not accepted. So that is probably something that you would need to change.

to make higher upfront costs more acceptable to executives and shareholders.

For sellers and their investment banks, the incentives can align differently. There, success fees can serve as a "healthy incentive" for the bankers, said Kirketerp-Moeller. "If you're successful in selling the company at a higher price than expected, then you get rewarded. But it also has its downsides. In companies where people are measured and paid based only on specific goals, then they tend to focus only on those goals and forget the rest."

However, the fact remains that it is still better for the investment bank to close a deal (perhaps selling the company at a discount) than risking that the transaction won't close by asking for too high a price. Similar incentives are found in other industries—for example, real estate brokers. So while alternatives to the success fee may look good in theory, in practice, the fee structure is very appealing to most corporations because they would rather not pay anything to their banks for a deal that isn't consummated.

The Benefits of In-House Valuations

Without question, investment banks can provide invaluable services, including intelligence, information, financial modeling, and sheer manpower (which can be critical for smaller clients). On the seller's side, "the big value of an investment bank is having access to potential buyers," said Stefan Wanjek, Head of M&A Economics at OMV AG. He opined that "They often know the potential buyers' universe better than we do here. They also may add value in terms of maximizing competition and optimizing the outcomes of negotiations."

In addition, bankers can help immunize clients against legal challenges if the deal falls apart, if the transaction later "goes south," or if the price is questioned. "If you hire a bank, you'll definitely get a faster M&A process because they are professionals at deal logistics and processing," said Ken Sasaki, Partner at TNT Capital LLC (Japan). He further pointed that "Internal M&A team is often understaffed with other responsibilities. Thus, it's helpful to be able to outsource the cumbersome due-diligence tasks. More manpower and experience are why banks speed up the process."

In recent years, though, the perceived value of hiring an investment bank has diminished as information becomes more readily available, independence is more highly prized, and corporate managers better understand the M&A process. In fact, the perceived utility of investment banks has fallen to the point where a significant minority of companies are eliminating them from M&As altogether. In 2017, for example, acquiring companies involved in public-company deals valued at more than $1 billion did *not* use a financial adviser in more than 25 percent of the cases. Comcast and AbbVie are among the big companies that recently decided to go "bank-less" during major acquisitions.[5] (*Note*: because of the potential for legal liability, it's more problematic for sellers to cut bankers out of the equation.)

Some executives attribute the rise of bank-less deals to a desire to keep transactions confidential, move quickly when needed, and save money. Others note that a growing number of companies are building internal M&A teams with the ability to develop deal strategy, create financial models, and execute transactions without the help of bankers. And, of course, I'm not the only person who observed that investment bankers may not always have clients' best interests at heart. No less a figure than Warren Buffet has accused bankers who "being paid as they are for action, constantly urge acquirers to pay 20% to 50% premiums over market price for publicly-held businesses…. A few years later, bankers – bearing straight faces – again appear and just as earnestly urge spinning off the earlier acquisition in order to 'unlock shareholder value.'"[6]

Roche Goes "Bank-less" to Buy Genentech

On March 12, 2009, the Swiss pharmaceutical giant Roche Holding announced a $46.8 billion deal to acquire the California-based biotech company Genentech. The path to the merger was long and tumultuous—one marked by a world economy in turmoil, by rejected offers and hostility between the parties, and by a high-risk gamble to finance the deal.

The relationship between Roche and Genentech dated to the 1980s when Genentech was a relatively new company that focused largely on the R&D of new products. (By contrast, Roche was founded in 1896 and had been present in the U.S. since 1905.) The Swiss firm employed more than 78,000 people at the time of its first takeover bid in 2008, while Genentech employed about 11,000. Genentech ended 2008 with a net income of more than $3.6 billion versus $9.33 billion for Roche. Genentech's net income for 2008 increased 14 percent over the previous year, while Roche experienced a 5 percent decline.[7]

In 1990, Roche bought 56 percent of Genentech for $2.1 billion, and in the years that followed, the biotech firm's product lines began to take off, with Genentech experiencing astronomical growth. Although partners on paper, Genentech's day-to-day operations were fully independent, with no significant collaboration between the two companies.

By 2008, Genentech's focus on R&D had waned, and the two companies frequently found themselves competing for the same deals and customers. In addition, an agreement that allowed Roche first rights to market Genentech drugs outside the U.S. was scheduled to end in 2015, and Roche was concerned that when it was time to renegotiate the deal, Genentech would demand a king's ransom for those rights or opt to sell the drugs overseas on its own.

On July 21, 2008, therefore, Roche went public with an offer of $43.7 billion ($89 a share) for the remaining stock of Genentech. Unfortunately, in terms of maintaining cordial relations, Genentech's leadership didn't learn about the offer until a few hours before the news media announced it.

Genentech rejected Roche's offer a month later as a substantial undervaluation of the company. Although this response was not a surprise, Roche's leaders were increasingly anxious to finalize the deal. The results of a clinical trial testing the effectiveness of a new cancer drug were due in April 2009, and if all went well, Genentech's share price might climb so high that it would put the deal out of Roche's reach.

Initially, Erich Hunziker, Roche's chief financial officer, faced a deluge of inquiries from investment banks that wanted to help finance the deal, on which their

(continued)

(continued)

upfront fees were expected to reach $250 million to $400 million. By mid-August 2008, however, a $45 billion syndicated bank facility seemed out of the question. After the collapse of Lehman Brothers in September, no bank wanted to build a syndicate with potentially vulnerable members. Interbank lending froze as banks focused on survival.

By early 2009, Hunziker was trying to figure out how Roche could borrow more than $40 billion to finance the buyout. With a syndicated bank loan no longer possible, Roche turned to the bond markets. But no company had ever issued such a large amount, and it seemed unlikely that Hunziker could persuade bond investors to finance such a huge transaction in such a short timeframe in the middle of the worst financial crisis since the Great Depression.

In response, Hunziker consulted with leading bond-rating agencies before scheduling a roadshow that took him around the world six times. Standard and Poor's (correctly) predicted a likely rating of AA—once the transaction closed, which gave Hunziker the ammunition he needed to convince potential investors. Thereafter, Roche completed three successful rounds of bond issuance in less than three weeks. In the first round in the U.S., Roche raised $19 billion at maturities ranging from 6 months to 30 years. This was the largest amount ever borrowed in the U.S. without the help of a bank or bank consortium. A week later, Roche raised €11.25 billion in Europe, and the next week a further CHF8 billion in Switzerland. These were also records. The total raised was approximately $42 billion.

Through its structuring of the deal and the elimination of the usual intermediaries, Roche reduced transaction costs by at least 50 percent and was able to allocate shorter- and longer-term bonds according to the needs of the company and bond investors. Eventually, Roche closed the Genentech acquisition. The final price came to $95 a share. Some analysts argued that the final offer was not a fair reflection of Genentech's long-term value, but also noted that the volatile market made the offer more attractive than it otherwise would have been.

*   *   *

Whenever possible, said most of my interviewees, companies should develop valuations in-house and with help from unbiased third-party advisers, whether or not they also hire an investment bank or banks. "The valuation has to be done in-house by the company," said Sandeep Jalan, CFO of Aperam SA. In his words,

I think the most important point is accountability … because investment advisers, once the deal is over, they go home. They're finished. It's the people who have promised the value and this or that synergy who will have to make that money. We need to have that accountability very clear. Who's going to deliver the promised value? [The investment advisers] are making nice projections and valuations, but who will deliver? An investment banker will never do that. It's not their job. Hence a strong internal attention to details of valuation and link to accountable persons to deliver is key.

For the managers of companies preparing for an M&A, therefore, it is critical to understand the key pillars of valuation and value creation. Otherwise, they will not be informed contributors to the discussion. Two key pillars are the stand-alone value of the target company and its value with synergies (discussed in more detail in Chap. 4). The others include:

- **Current market capitalization.** Typically, this is the lowest acceptable price that the target will accept (i.e., the "floor"). Indeed, it's unusual for the board of directors at the target company to agree to be purchased at a value per share that's lower than the current market price on the stock exchange. A premium is usually paid, and this premium should be seen as a function of the seller's value with synergies. In mergers with substantial synergies, the premium paid can be larger and still generate value for the acquirer.
- **Market multiples.** When valuing a company, it's common to analyze comparable companies' trading multiples as a benchmark. This involves analyzing various multiples at which companies in the same industry are trading. The main multiples used are enterprise value (EV) divided by earnings before interest, taxes, depreciation, and amortization (EBITDA) (the most common), the price-to-earnings ratio, and the price-to-book ratio. The logic behind a multiple analysis is to determine how much the market is currently paying for an asset with similar characteristics to the one being valued. Before using a multiple as a valuation benchmark, however, it's essential to identify a group of *truly* comparable companies and to consider the details of each one. It's also important to watch out for outliers, especially those with higher-than-average growth, higher margins, and lower risk. (A common mistake is blindly taking the average of the multiples of all companies in a given sector and then using this as a benchmark. Some of these firms won't be relevant peers.)
- **Transaction multiples.** It's not unusual to analyze, as a benchmark, comparable M&A transactions that have recently occurred in the same industry. This involves analyzing the multiples paid by the acquirers in the previous transactions. The more recent the deal, and the more similar the transaction to the one under consideration, the more relevant it is to the deal multiple. The same caveats apply to transaction multiples as to market multiples. In addition to an appropriate comparison group, it's important to consider the details of each transaction, including the potential for revenue and cost synergies, overlapping operations, and so on.
- **Previous premiums paid.** The final valuation method involves analyzing the premiums paid in previous (and similar) transactions. Here, the premium is usually defined as the offer price (how much the buyer is offering

per share of the target company) divided by the pre-announcement stock price of the target company. Because price "run-ups" may have occurred in the pre-announcement period (often due to information leaks), the premium is typically measured over the stock price for 30 days (or one week) prior to the announcement. (Again, it's important to consider the details of each previous transaction, as it is when using market and transaction multiples.)

Normally, discounted cash flow/net present value (DCF/NPV) should be the main valuation tool, but for small, non-public targets, we can expand the analysis to more basic tools, such as multiples of sales and so on. Ideally, valuing the target should be done by "triangulating" a range of values from different methodologies, for example, DCF and multiples. I always recommend using more than one method and one scenario, and then opting for a valuation *range* instead of a single number. From here, it's important to "stress test" assumptions using extreme scenarios.

Internal Teams Should Steer the M&A from A to Z

The internal M&A department should be the M&A "process owner," the group steering the transaction from Step A to Step Z. If no internal M&A department exists, then companies should create a specific project team with a clear leader, and this team should own the process and be accountable from A to Z. This requires that the company form the team well in advance and include business experts who will own the synergies post-closing. In addition, the team should include—or consult with—central function executives so these people can provide inputs into the valuation model. Although the internal team can be the only team developing the valuation, most of the executives with whom I consulted prefer to arrive at a final valuation in tandem with an external adviser or advisers (often an investment bank).

There are several ways to do this. At Dow Europe GMBH, for example, an investment bank might be hired to advise the company on the value of a transaction, and then Dow will "compare notes" with the valuation that it has generated internally. Stefan Koch, Director of M&As for Dow Europe, believes that both the company and the investment bank should be responsible for creating valuations. "The banker advises the client on the value of the transaction, and the client has to look at that advice with a critical eye," he said. "We try not to contaminate the bank's thinking about valuation when we ask them for one. We don't give them any guidance on what we think the right value is. But then we compare it with our own valuation based on our own metrics."

As an example, he added, Dow uses a certain discount factor, while banks typically use different discount rates, or a range of rates. "We also have some proprietary inputs into the valuation, based on synergy assumptions we might not want to share with the bank. So yeah, we use both valuations – the bank's valuation and our own." (Why not share those synergy assumptions with the bank? "Because some decisions are very confidential, and are based on strategies that wouldn't be appropriate to share with a third party, even our bank. Generally, the more the bank knows the better the advice they can give, but sometimes we just can't share certain things with an outside adviser.")

United Arab Emirates-based First Gulf Bank (FGB) adopted a similar approach during its successful 2013 acquisition of the credit card company Dubai First (DF). FGB had an internal valuation done, in addition to one by an external adviser. "We did our own internal valuation, and did not share anything with the company which gave us an idea on their valuation," said FGB chief financial officer Karim Karoui. "We took theirs without sharing with them, without influencing them. We gave a weight to all the points which they raised. We saw that they were very conservative and then putting a big weight on the provisionary requirements, things like that, on the portfolio. But when we took the decision at the end, we took it based on adding all the facts, adding our potential and then our ability to transform the company." This approach required that FGB have strong valuation skills in-house, as well as excellent collaboration between the different departments inside FGB.

Ultimately, it's up to senior managers, internal M&A teams, and boards to determine how, when, and whether to work with investment banks.

On the positive side, said Luciano Poli, CFO EMEAI and Finance Leader for JVs at Dow Europe, investment banks usually excel in due diligence, "making sure that you get the best view of what you are buying, including what liability you may be taking on from a Health, Safety and Environment (HSE) point of view, from a tax point of view, from a people point of view, and from a pension point of view." In addition, he pointed out that banks tend to be experienced and savvy negotiators, ensuring that their clients receive the most favorable terms and conditions.

On the negative side, "they give you enough rope for you to do something good or to hang yourself," said Poli. "When it comes to valuation, they are not there to say, 'I wouldn't do it.' Instead, if they see that you are convinced, they will often go along with you."

Ultimately, the question of whether an investment bank will add value, or contribute to its destruction, depends on the ability and willingness of the company's M&A team(s) to question assumptions and manage the bank's role. "The role of the investment bank is to execute, and my role is to manage and control and to take responsibility for the outcome of the deal," said Wanjek. He further added that "The investment bank plays a very important role if you manage it right."

Summary

Regardless of the merits, investment bankers are happy when deals close. It's the buyer's shareholders who bear the burden if the deal turns out to be a lemon. When a deal closes, the winner (or at least the happiest people) are investment banks, lawyers, the seller (otherwise, it would not close the deal), and the CEOs of both companies. The losers are typically the shareholders of the buyer. This is that is meant when I say that, on average, mergers destroy value.

Investment banks use league tables to promote themselves and display their rank. But league tables represent the values of the previous deals—not the *value creation* produced by those deals! Therefore, although investment banks are a necessary part of most M&A transactions, companies should never rely on them to provide a final valuation and negotiate the deal because of the inherent conflict of interest stemming from their fee structure. The "success fee" gives them a powerful incentive to close every deal. Investment bankers are people—people whose business is maximizing profits from the sale of their services. Advising *against* deals is not in their interests.

According to most executives interviewed for this book, some *individual* bankers are *always on the side of the deal,* while others are more likely to protect their clients' interests. But in general, there is considerable incentive for banks to maximize their fees. More than one executive noted, however, that any bank putting its own interests ahead of the client's will probably not be invited to participate in future deals.

One way to reduce or eliminate the perverse incentives for banks would be to pay them higher retainers and lower success fees, but ironically, many companies balk at this because it transfers the risk to them (of paying a big fee for a deal that might not close). The dynamics are often different on the seller's side. There, the higher the value at which the company is sold, the higher the banks' fees. But the fact remains that it is still better for the investment bank to close a deal, perhaps selling at a discount, than to risk not closing it by asking for too high a price.

So, why should companies hire investment banks? Banks can provide valuable resources, including intelligence, financial modeling, and sheer manpower (for smaller clients). However, their value is decreasing as information becomes more available, independence is more valued, and managers better understand M&As. In fact, the perceived value of the banks has fallen to the point where a significant number of companies are eliminating them from M&As altogether.

Whenever possible, companies should develop the valuations in-house or with the aid of third-party advisers who are less likely to be biased for or against the deal. For the managers of companies preparing for an M&A, therefore, it is critical to understand the key pillars of valuation and value creation. Otherwise, they will not be informed contributors to the discussion.

Normally, discounted cash flow/net present value (DCF/NPV) should be the main valuation tool, but for small, non-public targets, we can expand the analysis to more basic tools, like multiples of sales and so on. Valuing companies should be done by triangulating a range of values from different methodologies: DCF and multiples. Use more than one method and one scenario and opt for a valuation range instead of a single number. Be sure to stress test all assumptions using extreme scenarios.

The internal M&A department should be the M&A "process owners," the group steering the transaction from A to Z. This requires that the company form the team well in advance and include business experts who will own the synergies post-closing. In addition, the team should include—or consult with—central function executives so they can provide inputs into the valuation model. Although the internal team can be the only team developing the valuation, many executives prefer to develop a final valuation in tandem with an external adviser(s). Developing a valuation internally also helps to promote buy-in and accountability.

Questions for Executives Considering Future M&As

- Would you be willing to spend more on bank fees upfront (and risk that the deal might not close) in exchange for more objective advice and lower fees after a successful closing?
- Is your internal M&A equipped (in terms of human resources and expertise) to develop accurate valuations?

- Is your company willing to hire independent external advisers to evaluate a proposed transaction? (*Note*: the pay for these advisers must be non-contingent on the deal's outcome.)
- Do most of your managers understand the key pillars of valuation and value creation?
- In previous M&A transactions, do you believe that your firm was well-served (in terms of accurate and objective guidance) from its external advisers?
- Would you ever consider cutting investment banks out of an M&A transaction altogether?
- Are the synergies quantified in the proposed M&A? How do they relate to the premium paid?

Notes

1. Arik Hesseldahl, "HP's $5 Billion Fraud Lawsuit against Former Autonomy Executives Is Now Public." *Recode*, May 5, 2015.
2. Michael Bobelian, "HP's $8.8 Billion Fiasco Exposes Flaws in M&A Process." *Forbes*, November 21, 2012.
3. By Nadia Damouni and Nicola Leske, "In HP-Autonomy debacle, many advisers but little good advice." Reuters.com, November 21, 2012.
4. Ibid.
5. Dana Mattioli, "An Investment Banker's Worst Nightmare; More companies are deciding to do without bankers when they make acquisitions." *The Wall Street Journal*, May 10, 2016.
6. Ibid.
7. http://knowledge.wharton.upenn.edu/article/anatomy-of-a-merger-hostile-deals-become-friendly-in-the-end-right/

2

Avoid "Strategic" Deals

In the final year of the twentieth century, a telecommunications giant was born when Vodafone AirTouch acquired Mannesmann AG in a hostile, all-stock deal worth £112 billion, creating the world's fourth-largest company (valued at £224 billion).

Just six years later, Vodafone achieved another, more dubious, distinction when it recorded the largest loss in European history, writing off £23.5 billion connected to the acquisition.[1] It was an embarrassing admission that Vodafone had grossly overpaid for Mannesmann. Although the purchase had been labeled strategic, it was instead "strategic"—an M&A in which the target's valuation with synergies did not justify the premium paid.

Based in the U.K., Vodafone had become the world's largest mobile tele-communications company by 1999. As it grew, the company pursued a "mobile-only" expansion strategy, rather than combining mobile and fixed networks. The strategy had proven successful for the company and its share-holders. Sales and operating profits of continuing operations were up 34 percent and 17 percent, respectively, for the six months leading to September 1999 over a similar period in the previous year.[2]

By comparison, Mannesmann AG was a relatively new player in the tele-communications industry. It began life in 1890 as a producer of seamless steel tubes and entered the telecom industry in 1990 when it established D2, the first private mobile phone network in Germany. Although late to the game, Mannesmann quickly became one of Europe's largest telecommunications firms by following an integrated (rather than a mobile-only) strategy that focused on the European market. The two companies were indirect partners through their stakes in Cegetel, D2, OPI, and Mannesmann Arcor.

© The Author(s) 2019
N. Fernandes, *The Value Killers*, https://doi.org/10.1007/978-3-030-12216-4_2

While some in the news media were speculating that Mannesmann was ripe for a takeover, the event that incited Vodafone's acquisition bid occurred in October 1999 when Mannesmann CEO Dr. Klaus Esser announced that his company had acquired Orange PLC, one of Vodafone's chief rivals in the U.K. market. On November 14, Vodafone CEO Chris Gent responded by writing a letter to Esser in which he summarized the strategic case for merging their two companies and offered to pay 43.7 Vodafone shares for each Mannesmann share. The offer was rejected as inadequate.

On November 19, Vodafone announced an amended offer that would provide 53.7 shares of Vodafone stock for every share of Mannesmann. This would have granted 47.2 percent of the merged company to the target's shareholders and valued Mannesmann at about €232 per share—a 55 percent premium over Mannesmann's share price before takeover speculation began.

The Mannesmann board advised shareholders (on that same day) to reject the offer, with Esser claiming the company was worth €350 a share. Henceforth, the takeover bid turned hostile, with Gent determining that, to acquire Mannesmann, he would have to convince the latter's shareholders that a Vodafone-Mannesmann merger would better serve their interests than the combination of Orange and Mannesmann.

On February 3, 2000, however, Esser accepted a revised offer of 58.9646 Vodafone shares for every Mannesmann share, giving his company's shareholders a 49.5 percent stake in the newly combined firm. This translated into a valuation for Mannesmann of €180 billion—or €350 per share at the prices prevailing on that day. In other words, Vodafone gave Esser the exact valuation he'd claimed for Mannesmann—a valuation that, back in November, had elicited expressions of disbelief from Vodafone's management. The final price paid was 75 percent above the first offer from Vodafone and reflected a premium of more than 130 percent relative to Mannesmann's share price prior to the deal.

For completing the transaction, Vodafone gave Gent a bonus of £5 million in shares and £5 million in cash. (Other Vodafone directors also received bonuses of £5 million.) This decision generated shareholder anger, especially after Vodafone's share price fell by 15 percent. Meanwhile, Esser was criticized (and sued) for receiving $30 million in severance pay (but he eventually prevailed in the lawsuit).

Although this deal proved to be a failure of AOL-Time Warner proportions (see below)—and to some observers it appeared like a misguided attempt to acquire Orange by swallowing the fish that swallowed another fish—it should be noted that a Vodafone-Mannesmann merger was not entirely without merit. Significant revenue-enhancement and cost-saving synergies were identified. For example, the Vodafone board estimated that synergies from the voice business would be around £500 million in 2003 and £600 million in 2004. In 2003, revenue growth, cost savings, and savings on capital expenditures were expected to account for approximately 20 percent, 40 percent, and 40 percent of the savings, respectively.[3] Although the size of these synergies can be debated, as can the assumptions underlying them, there's no reason to believe that they were fictional. However, any reasonable valuation of the synergies would never come close to the price paid. By overpaying for the asset, Vodafone destroyed whatever value the merger might have produced, transforming what could have been a value-creating purchase into the type of acquisition that I call "strategic."

"Strategic" Is a Dangerous Word

All too often, the word "strategic" is a euphemism used by the deal champion who cannot justify the proposed transaction with quantifiable facts. In fact, the term has become so synonymous with vague or unsound rationales that many of the experts interviewed for this book had an immediate, negative response to the question, *What is your first reaction when a deal is justified as strategic?* "When you say the deal is strategic, it usually means you are overpaying," said Jordi Costa, VP, Agribusiness, Sugar & Bioenergy, at Bunge SA. "It means you don't have enough hard synergies or a strong enough business case to justify it for certain. If the deal were less 'strategic,' you'd be able to put [the rationale] into words and numbers."

Stefan Wanjek of OMV AG said he is "skeptical" of any deal that is characterized as strategic. "You have to very carefully examine the definition of strategic value then. I know people can become very creative ... but 'strategic acquisition' often is the final argument."

Said Michael Jeppesen, CFO of Solar A/S Group, "When a deal is called strategic, or the costs are strategic or the initiatives are strategic, I get nervous. Sometimes they become strategic after they turn out to be bad deals. Maybe I'm being cynical, or maybe I just have too much experience, but I think management has an incentive to buy things. I think it's in the genes of CEOs. They want to buy, build and expand, and sometimes that happens even at the expense of value creation."

In theory, there's nothing wrong with labeling a deal a "strategic acquisition." In practice, however, some deal champions default to this phrase whenever they wish to mask their true motivations, which are sometimes based on ego and emotion rather than facts. This is why "strategic" has become a euphemism for deals that lack *genuine strategic logic*—that is, deals in which estimates of "hard" and "soft" synergies have not been accurately quantified and the assumptions underlying them rigorously tested (see Chap. 4). Instead, vague statements such as "nobody else can do this" or "if we don't do this, the competition will" are commonly heard in support of "strategic deals" and are a sign of trouble.

InBev-Anheuser-Busch: A Cost-Cutting Success Story

As a rule, cost-saving synergies are more often realized than revenue-enhancement synergies—if only because acquirers have more control over cost-cutting measures than they do revenue generation. (It's easier to shutter plants, reduce a workforce, and eliminate operational redundancies than convince customers to buy more products.) This was certainly the case following the acquisition of St. Louis-based Anheuser-Busch by InBev—a deal finalized in July 2008 when the Belgian company paid $52 billion for the U.S. firm to create the world's largest beer brewer.

In the decade leading up to the merger, worldwide sales of beer had been growing slowly, and the industry was consolidating in the face of rising commodity prices (barley, malt, hops, glass, and aluminum) in an effort to achieve greater economies of scale. Since 2003, the industry has witnessed 883 M&A deals with an estimated value of $200 billion. Among the biggest deals was the 2004 purchase of Miller by South African Breweries, which created SABMiller, and the merger of Belgium's Interbrew with Brazil-based AmBev, which gave rise to InBev.[4]

Although an InBev merger with Anheuser-Busch (AB) promised cost savings in terms of production and brand portfolio, as well as shared best practices in cost management, the limited market overlap between the companies suggested that these synergies might be minimal. What's more, InBev's "pay-for-performance" culture could not have been more at odds with AB's "perks-regardless-of-performance" culture. A clash was inevitable, and it came faster than expected.

One day after the acquisition became official, Carlos Brito, the new AB InBev CEO, flew to St. Louis to address AB's management. Although AB had arranged for him to stay at the Ritz-Carlton hotel, Brito—who had flown commercial—opted to stay at the Holiday Inn, a moderately priced hotel. AB executives were accustomed to lavish perks such as AirBud—the fleet of 6 planes, 2 helicopters, and 20 pilots that ferried them to business meetings—first-class hotels, and $1000 business meals. By contrast, InBev executives flew coach class, stayed in three-star hotels (sometimes sharing rooms), and ate modestly priced meals.[5]

Brito's choice of hotel was merely the symbolic start of things to come.

InBev pledged to eliminate $1.5 billion in costs at AB within three years. The savings would come from synergies, such as better negotiating power with suppliers, manufacturing improvements, optimization of supply chain, sharing best practices, and increased cross-selling. Most of them did not require massive layoffs (three weeks after the merger, 1400 workers were laid off, which represented only six percent of the AB workforce, with another 1000 employees taking early retirement).

(continued)

(continued)

The combined company even reduced costs at the expense of product quality. For example, it decided to limit the use of high-quality hops from the Hallertau region of Germany with less expensive (and less flavorful) hops, and to stop importing the Beck's brand of beer from Germany and instead brew it in the U.S. (where production would no longer be governed by Germany's famous purity laws).

Although some customers protested the changes, InBev management correctly predicted that what mattered most was what consumers *bought*, not what they said. And consumers continued to buy the company's beers. In 2014, AB InBev had 18 percent of global beer sales and one-third of the profits. Moreover, InBev's cost-cutting target was not only met but was exceeded by $750 million. In addition, the company sold $9 billion in AB assets, including its ten amusement parks and its stake in China's Tsingtao beer. These actions allowed Brito and his team to achieve in three years—instead of five—an ambitious debt-reduction goal, triggering generous bonuses for 40 eligible AB InBev managers.

InBev's approach to cost reduction was painful, but the patient survived and emerged healthier than ever. Two years after the deal, more than $2.2 billion of synergies had been achieved (more than anticipated and faster than planned), and InBev stock price rose steadily, reflecting the value creation of the deal. Three years after the closing, in spite of the 2008 financial crisis, the stock price was twice what it had been prior to the AB acquisition.

Good and Bad Reasons for Doing Deals

There are many good reasons for doing deals—for example, increasing the company's product line, broadening distribution, and reducing unit costs. Carlos Ghosn, former CEO of Renault Nissan, summarized "Synergies are not only about cost reduction. Synergies can be access to markets, exchange of products, avoiding overlaps, exchange of best practices."[6]

Unfortunately, there are just as many bad reasons for initiating M&As, and these reasons are rarely quantifiable. Most often, the bad reasons are associated with achieving greater diversification and size. It should go without saying, however, that larger size doesn't guarantee better company performance (nor a higher CEO salary) and neither does growth for growth's sake (as opposed to growth for the sake of growing profits).

What the bad reasons tend to have in common is that they are frequently the product of CEO ego and overconfidence. Another common trait, according to Alan Lewis and Dan McKone,[7] is that bad rationales often ignore the customer's desires. To identify a good deal, they believe, executives should ask what "permission" their customers would give them to extend their current products to help customers achieve their "ultimate mission." For example, the success of the 2005 merger of Procter & Gamble (P&G) and Gillette came about not just because the new organization achieved certain cost synergies, but because P&G combined its Mach blade technology with its women's skin care expertise to market women's shaving products under Gillette's Venus brand. Meanwhile, Gillette introduced new shave lotions, deodorants, and shower gels for men using P&G's technology and know-how. In other words, each company leveraged the other's resources to better serve their existing customer bases with new or enhanced beauty products. The acquisition made sense for P&G and Gillette because it made sense for their customers.

In contrast, Lewis and McKone point to eBay's acquisition of Skype as an example of a deal that failed because eBay management misidentified the "journey" that its customers wanted to take. eBay executives believed its customers would grant them permission to add video chat to the core offering—online auctions. But as it turned out, eBay customers were largely uninterested in using video chat to assist their auction businesses and, even when they *were* interested, they didn't care whether eBay provided the service. For this reason, the deal's main rationale—the potential cross-selling synergy—did not materialize.

Although the Lewis-McKone approach has merit, especially when it comes to identifying revenue-enhancement synergies, there are some obvious exceptions to the "customer permission" theory. For example, AB's customers certainly did *not* grant the combined company permission to downgrade the quality of AB's beers in an effort to save money. In fact, some of them objected very loudly, yet the deal was an unqualified success from AB InBev's point of view.

As a rule, M&As that are justified on the basis of projected revenue increases should be approached with caution (see Chap. 4 for "hard" and "soft" synergies). In fact, one of the executives interviewed shared a case history that illustrates this very point:

Prior to the merger, Company A had a 14 percent market share and Company B had a market share of 11 percent. In theory, therefore, the combined company should have enjoyed a 25 percent market share. In this case, however, the acquirer projected additional revenue synergies based on bundling of complementary products, price increases, and so on, which caused it to predict a market share of 30 percent within two years of the closing.

Unfortunately, reality was not as kind to the new company as the estimates—a result that frequently occurs whenever deals are undertaken in the hope of increasing revenues. Instead of capturing 30 percent of the market, the newly merged company achieved just 20 percent—for one simple reason. Post-deal, many of the firms' former customers sought out alternative suppliers for fear of becoming too dependent on a single company. So, in the end, a combined company ended up selling far fewer products than its stand-alone predecessors. (See Chap. 5 for more information on the risks of employee and customer attrition during and after M&As, and what organizations can do to mitigate the risks.)

Microsoft's Effort to Buy Yahoo: An Irrational Target?

So far, the case studies we've examined have focused on acquirers. But buyers are not the only people who can behave irrationally. Sellers can also make "strategic" decisions that cost their shareholders dearly. Typically, this "strategy" takes the form of refusing to sell when the price is right—or even generous. For example: On January 31, 2008, Yahoo CEO Jerry Yang received a letter from Microsoft CEO Steve Balmer in which the latter offered to acquire Yahoo at a 62 percent premium above that day's closing price of $19.18 per share. Under the proposal's terms, Microsoft would purchase all outstanding shares of Yahoo common stock for $31 apiece, payable in cash or 0.9509 of a share of Microsoft common stock.[8] Balmer pointed to his company's strong revenue and earnings growth, as well as synergies that included economies of scale, expanded R&D capacity, and operational efficiencies, as the rationales for the merger.

On February 11, 2008, after months of lobbying by Yang (which included convincing the board to guarantee extremely expensive severance for any employees laid-off in the event of a change in control), Yahoo's board rejected the offer as a substantial undervaluation.

In response, Balmer sent a second letter (on April 5), suggesting that, in light of the deteriorating US economy and other factors, Microsoft's initial offer should be viewed as increasingly attractive. He also warned that if the board didn't accept the offer in three weeks, Microsoft would go directly to Yahoo's shareholders, "including the initiation of a proxy contest to elect an alternative slate of directors for the Yahoo board."[9]

Yang rejected this second overture, stating that Microsoft had failed to enter into meaningful negotiations with his company, though he claimed Yahoo remained open to a transaction with Microsoft if the price was right.

Balmer eventually raised the offer to $33 per share, but this was also rejected, with Yang reportedly saying that he wouldn't take anything less than $37 per share. In early May, Microsoft walked away from the deal.

In the aftermath of the failed deal, Yahoo stock plummeted, dropping to less than $10 per share by November 2008[10] and the company was later sold for less than 20 percent of what Microsoft had offered. Yang resigned as CEO shortly thereafter.

Did Yang's refusal to sell the company rise to the level of "irrational" behavior? The answer depends on whom you ask—and when.

In the short term, a source of potential shareholder value was destroyed because of his actions. By 2013, though, Yahoo stock finally surpassed the price that Microsoft was willing to pay, and it has risen further since then—thanks, in part, to Yang's decision (in 2005) to invest in a Chinese startup venture called

(continued)

Boards Can Prevent Bad Deals

Because boards of directors play a critical role in all mergers, joint ventures, and strategic alliances, they can—and should—serve as a check against misguided M&As. In the vast majority of M&As, the deal is proposed by senior management and then submitted to the board for consideration. Ideally, the directors will be well-positioned to contain CEO overconfidence and emotions, and ensure that the focus stays on fact-based discussions about value creation. It will concentrate on the potential risks and rewards of the transaction and provide a strategic framework for decisions, as well as guidelines for the board's level of participation in the process. Specifically, the board should:

- Ask the deal champion(s), the key questions WHY-WHERE-HOW: "Why should we do a deal with this particular company at this particular time? Where is the value, and how will we capture it?"
- Confirm that the value added is sufficient to outweigh the costs, risks, and staff resources.
- Challenge and understand the potential points of risk, and ensure that management has appropriate mechanisms in place to mitigate those risks.
- Develop a discussion and negotiation framework to govern management's actions.
- Understand how valuations are performed, and what the key assumptions are, and be able to question them.
- Determine how success will be measured, and how management proposes to report on its progress.
- Ask how problems that arise during the process will be managed.

In reality, not all boards, and board members, are able to fulfill their critical role. The board's ability to serve as a devil's advocate depends on its composition, degree of independence, governance mechanisms, and on the actual knowledge and expertise of the individual members.

For example, one study concluded that "independent outside directors enhance target shareholder gains from tender offers, and that boards with a majority of independent directors are more likely to use resistance strategies to enhance shareholder wealth."[11]

On the buyer side, another study concluded that having financial experts on boards of directors significantly affects corporate decisions, though not necessarily in the interest of shareholders. Among other things, it found that having investment bankers on the board tends to produce larger bond issues, but worse acquisitions.[12]

In some instances, however, the effectiveness of outside directors may be compromised by lack of industry knowledge and attention, said Ken Sasaki of TNT Capital LLC (Japan).

> There are many outside directors nowadays at the board, but they sometimes lack basic industry knowledge to engage in meaningful discussions. An outside director being a board member of multiple companies can also be a limitation.

Overconfidence is another factor that can affect the ability of the board to check the chief executive's desire to close a deal at any cost. Over the years, CEO overconfidence has been studied by numerous researchers, which have documented its detrimental impact on shareholder value creation. Also known as the "winner's curse," overconfident CEOs operate under the influence of confirmation bias or "self-attribution bias"—the tendency to attribute positive outcomes to their own abilities and ascribe failures to external circumstances or third parties. The evidence indicates that, over time, executives afflicted with overconfidence engage in M&A transactions that produce significantly lower returns to the shareholders than their first few deals. In other words, the successful M&As that helped fuel their overconfidence later prompt them to pursue riskier and riskier ventures that are more likely to destroy value.

Incentives matter. Having *skin in the game* typically leads to better decisions. One research study also found that managers are more likely to engage in unnecessary mergers when they own a smaller share of their company, either directly or through compensation packages,[13] while a second uncovered a strong positive relation between acquiring managers' equity-based compensation and the stock price performance around the acquisition announcement.[14]

Like managers, board members are also human, so it should come as no surprise that they may also suffer from confirmation-bias-induced overconfidence. Axel Kind and Torsten Twardawski have discovered, for example, a "robust" correlation between the premiums paid for acquisitions and the level of board overconfidence. In fact, "acquisition premiums rise by 3.16 percentage points on average if the fraction of overconfident directors on the board is increased by 10%."[15]

With this in mind, companies might be wise to appoint outside advisers to help the board serve as a more thorough counterweight to the CEO and other senior managers spearheading the deal. Halbart Völker of NIBC Bank noted that "boards are often not qualified to have a discussion about valuations or deal rationales, or a combination of valuation and rationale [while most] management teams are well prepared and have the benefit of being more skillful and knowledgeable in those respects. So sometimes you see boards being assisted by a separate adviser to the board."

Without a doubt, boards need to have both the independence and skills to understand and identify synergies and, in some cases, develop valuations and value-creating strategies. Toward that end, they should be allowed to hire independent professionals and/or teams to provide advice regarding the valuation and upside/downside potential of the transaction. Relying entirely on a management presentation of the risks and rewards can put directors in a position of dependency—hardly a good place for a devil's advocate.

By the way, payment for advice provided to the board should *not* take the form of a success fee. The overall sum should be the same, whether the deal is done or not. (See Chap. 1 on the problems of success-based fees.)

AOL-Time Warner: The Archetypal "Strategic" Deal

When America Online announced on January 10, 2000, that it was acquiring Time Warner for about $182 billion in stock and debt, the news media (and many others) widely hailed the transaction as "visionary" and "transformative." Most observers declared that the merger, the largest in US history (valued at $350 billion), had created the "company of the future," signaling the official dawn of the digital media era.

Only a few months after the deal closed, however, the dot.com bubble burst and the US economy went into recession. Soon thereafter, advertising dollars began drying up, and AOL was forced to take a write-off of about $99 billion in 2002. The company also began losing subscribers and subscription revenue, thanks largely to the competitive advantages of the much faster broadband (versus AOL's increasingly antiquated dial-up service), which helped send the company's stock into free fall. The total value of AOL plummeted within a few years, dropping from $226 billion to $20 billion.[16]

Today, the AOL-Time Warner merger is universally derided as the worst deal in history. To say that the deal destroyed shareholder value is an understatement. "Obliterated" is a more accurate term. By the 10th year anniversary of the deal,

(continued)

(continued)

the combined value of the two companies (which had separated by then) was about one-seventh of their worth on the date of the merger.[17]

This isn't to say that the deal was not "visionary." After all, Gerald M. Levin (former head of Time Warner) and AOL co-founder Stephen M. Case *did* correctly predict that the Internet would soon demolish the traditional business models of mainstream media businesses. But vision is not the same as strategic logic, so the multi-million dollar question is: What was the rationale for *this particular* deal? And given the catastrophic results, where was the due diligence, did anyone challenge the deal, and why was the integration so poorly executed?

On the surface, the rationale made some sense. Before talks began between the CEOs of the two companies, both executives sought a foothold in the other's industry. Flush with cash, AOL had been shopping around for a traditional media company, while Time Warner had been seeking to establish an online presence. By combining the two companies, Time Warner would acquire tens of millions of new subscribers for its cable TV and print content. AOL would also gain access to new customers and add its digital media capabilities to the mix. Both CEOs were excited about the deal, and neither of these men were dummies.

Unfortunately, the due diligence appears to have been somewhat perfunctory and, what's more, many executives of Time Warner and AOL were not notified of the transaction until a few hours before the announcement—and in some cases, not until the very day of the announcement.

Some of these managers were not pleased with the news. Don Logan, then head of Time Inc., later said the deal was "the dumbest idea I had ever heard in my life." Timothy A. Boggs, then head of government relations at Time Warner, was more explicit. "I knew and I loved Time Warner. I saw it as a company with a vision and a set of values, and I saw AOL in a much less favorable light, much more opportunistic, made up of folks who were really trying to merely exploit the market they were in as opposed to developing something that was enduring, and I was very leery about this deal."[18]

Bogg's concerns foreshadowed the corporate culture clash to come. This culture war caused at least one disgruntled manager to leak damaging information about AOL to the media, which eventually prompted the Securities and Exchange Commission and the Justice Department to launch investigations into allegations that AOL had improperly inflated its advertising revenues. In the end, the company was forced to pay significant fines and to restate its past earnings, but as we now know, that turned out to be the least of its problems.

It's Not the CEO's Job to Diversify the Company's Portfolio

Although it's easy to blame Case and Levin today for the disastrous outcome of the merger, they are not entirely at fault. For example, they could not have predicted the massive drop in advertising revenues caused by the sudden bursting of the dot.com bubble. That being said, AOL should have been more concerned about the potential for high-speed broadband to render its dial-up technology obsolete. And if the merger was an attempt, even in part, to achieve greater diversification on behalf of the shareholders, it should never have been undertaken in the first place. It's not the job of chief executives to diversify their firm's portfolios on behalf of shareholders. Shareholders can achieve diversification for themselves with far less risk.

Even if diversification was not one of the rationales for the deal, it appears obvious that neither Case nor Levin did a good job of winning the hearts and minds of their senior managers for the deal. And in the absence of buy-in from different business and functional managers, there will be less account-ability for achieving synergies. For any deal to be successful, cost, revenue, and financial synergies must be identified and quantified. The acquirer must know when, how, and *who* is responsible for achieving them. In other words, the acquirer has to appoint synergy owners who know what to deliver, as well as *when* and *how* to deliver it. (See Chap. 3 for more details.)

Again, I'm not demanding that the word *strategic* be banned from every-one's lexicon—only that the word not be abused. To do this, it's important to know what the strategic rationale is and how to translate it into numbers and key performance indicators (KPIs). When making the case for a deal, there-fore, the word "strategic" should be part of a specific statement, and it should always be followed by the word **because**—for example, "This merger is Strategic **because** ...." The "because" should then outline the deal's key busi-ness drivers and benefits—drivers and benefits that, in most cases, can be quantified and logically justified.

Red Flags and Green Flags

There are a number of warning signs that a deal billed as strategic may, in fact, be "strategic":

- The CEO is the only person who believes in the deal.
- The synergies analysis focuses on revenue enhancement rather than cost savings.
- Cultural due diligence is not done or is performed superficially.
- The acquirer has done few deals and hasn't sought external expertise.
- The price limit (the internally set walk-away price) continually changes during the bidding phase.

- There are a number of bidders competing for the target.
- At some stage of the M&A, the deal is defended by pointing out how much time, money, or prestige has already been invested in the deal (sunk costs).
- The deal champions are determined to finalize the transaction at any cost.
- There are no mechanisms to have teams or managers challenging the deal in an open fashion.

Encountering one or more of these red flags should (at a minimum) cause the participants to slow down and re-evaluate the deal.

In addition to red flags, there are at least two "green flags," said some of the executives I interviewed. These indicate that, in many cases, the parties are probably on the right track.

According to Marcus Hanana of Procter & Gamble, one green flag is to "focus on key inputs. 'What happens to my market share if I buy this brand? What happens to my customer base?' You need to invest in a better customer experience, in a better product, in higher quality before making calculations on the financial revenue and the ROI."

For Jordi Costa of Bunge SA, a good green-light rationale revolves around significant cost-saving synergies. "We try to define what the hard synergies and soft synergies are. Hard synergies, for instance, are about costs – when we're able to pool procurement, and thanks to the acquisition, buy cheaper natural gas. When we get more bargaining power and we're going to be able to lower the price of everything. Synergies that involve more market share or increasing revenues or being able to increase the price of what we sell ... we often don't realize them."

"Another variable, whose presence is an often-overlooked green flag (and whose absence might be a red flag) is the purchase agreement itself," according to Luciano Poli of Dow Europe. "In my experience, a very good purchase or sale agreement is very important. It's critical to make sure that all the key terms and conditions are properly evaluated because all those details described in the agreement can create (or destroy) a lot of value – things like environmental liability, EH&S, etc. These things are extremely important in our business."

Although the presence of red flags doesn't necessarily mean the deal is a lemon and the presence of green flags doesn't guarantee a winner, these flags *can* offer valuable clues about the wisdom of moving forward with the M&A. At the very least, do not ignore them.

Summary

"Strategic" is a dangerous word. Too often, the term is used when a deal cannot be justified with quantifiable facts. There are many good reasons for doing deals—for example, increasing the company's product line, broadening distribution, reducing unit costs, and so on. There are also many bad reasons for doing deals, and these are rarely quantifiable. Bad reasons are often associated with diversification and size, as well as CEO ego, emotion, and overconfidence (especially self-attribution bias). To identify a good deal, based on revenue synergies, executives should ask themselves what "permission" their customers would give them to extend their current products to help customers achieve their "ultimate mission."

But just as acquirers can sometimes behave emotionally, so can sellers. Yahoo CEO Jerry Yang's rejection of Microsoft's 2008 acquisition bid is one example of this. Yang irrationally rejected Microsoft's offer, and shareholders paid a heavy price.

Boards should play a significant role in preventing the approval of bad deals. Boards can do this by containing CEO overconfidence and ego, bringing the discussion back to facts and value creation. Key questions that a board should always ask include: "Why an M&A? Why XYZ company? Why now? Where is the value from this deal, and how will we capture it?" To serve as a check on deal champions, however, directors need to possess both skill and independence. Where knowledge and expertise are lacking, they should be allowed to hire independent help to advise them on the valuation and potential of the deal. However, the independent advice should not be paid in the form of a success fee.

Diversification can be achieved by shareholders at little cost in financial markets, so it's not the job of CEOs to pursue diversification. Advocates of such deals tend to use the word "strategic" to justify them, but when a CEO says, "This is strategic," it's usually a bad sign. The classic example of a "strategic" deal is the merger of Time Warner and AOL in 2000.

It's key that synergies be clearly identified, quantified, and that the acquirer knows when, how, and who is going to achieve them if the deal is to be successful. Moreover, when estimating synergies, one needs to recruit hearts and minds. That is why getting buy-in from different business and functional managers is important.

It's not that the word "strategic" cannot be used, but that it shouldn't be abused. It's important to know where the strategic rationale is and how to translate that into numbers and KPIs. And people should be held accountable on these forecasted numbers later on. Make sure all rationales are specific and use the word *because*—for example, "this merger is strategic *because* ...." They should also illustrate the deal's key business drivers and benefits, which can be quantified in most cases.

There are a number of common red flags that suggest that anticipated synergies from the M&A will not occur—at least, not on schedule. There are also green flags that often indicate that the deal is on the right track. While the presence of red flags doesn't necessarily translate into a bad deal and the presence of green flags doesn't guarantee a winner, these flags *can* offer valuable clues about the wisdom of moving forward with a proposed M&A.

Questions for Future M&As

- Have you ever used the word "strategic" to describe a proposed M&A?
- Have you participated in a deal that was initiated for bad reasons?
- Does your company keep customers in mind when researching/planning M&As?
- Has your company's board of directors ever questioned, or helped kill, a deal?
- Does the board typically retain outside advisers to assist them independently with assessing an M&A?
- Do the projected synergies tend to focus on reduced costs or increased revenues?
- Is the board of directors receiving enough information and time to analyze the deal?
- Is there "deal fever"—key managers determined to finalize the transaction at all costs?
- Does the board of directors have the necessary skills to evaluate a deal?
- Do you have the right incentives in place, to make sure managers have "skin in the game," or are accountable for their proposals?

Notes

1. "Vodafone records largest loss in European history – shares rise." *The Register*, June 2, 2006.
2. "Vodafone AirTouch's Bid for Mannesmann." Harvard Business School, August 22, 2003.
3. Ibid.

4. Nuno Fernandes, "Big Beer: InBev vs. Anheuser-Busch." IMD, 2010.
5. John Weeks, "AB InBev: Dream, People, Culture, and Cost." IMD, 2015.
6. Wall Street Journal. July 13, 2006. http://online.wsj.com/articles/SB115282069310906058, accessed March 18, 2015.
7. Alan Lewis and Dan McKone, "So Many M&A Deals Fail Because Companies Overlook This Simple Strategy." *Harvard Business Review*, May 10, 2016.
8. Wei Jiang, "Microsoft's Attempt to Acquire Yahoo: A Case in Letters." Columbia Business School, November 14, 2012.
9. Ibid.
10. Nicholas Carlson, "Jerry Lang Laughs Last: 5 Years Later, Yahoo's Share Price Finally Exceeds Microsoft's Final Offer." BusinessInside, October 23, 2013.
11. James F. Cotter, Anil Shivdasani, Marc Zenner, "Do independent directors enhance target shareholder wealth during tender offers?" *Journal of Financial Economics*, February 1997.
12. A. Burak Güner, Ulrike Malmendier, Geoffrey Tate, "Financial Expertise of Directors." NBER Working Paper No. 11914, January 2006.
13. Michael C. Jensen and William H. Meckling, "Theory of the Firm: Managerial Behavior, Agency Costa and Ownership Structure." *Journal of Financial Economics*, 1976.
14. Datta, S., M. Iskandar-Datta, and K. Raman (2001). Executive compensation and corporate acquisition decisions. *Journal of Finance* 56(6), 2299–2336.
15. Axel Kind and Torsten Twardawsski, "Board Overconfidence in Mergers & Acquisitions: A Self-Attribution Bias." 2016.
16. Rita Gunther McGrath, "15 years later, lessons from the failed AOL-Time Warner merger." *Fortune*, January 10, 2015.
17. "How the AOL-Time Warner Deal Went Wrong." *The New York Times*, January 11, 2010.
18. Ibid.

3

Link the Before and After

The success of an M&A is about more than identifying synergies and developing a competitive valuation for the target. It's about knowing which people to involve—*and when*—in order to actually capture the synergies and justify that valuation. From the outset, therefore, it is vital for the acquiring company to implement a well-integrated, continuous process linking the pre-deal phase to the deal period and the post-deal integration.

The bad news is that many companies underestimate the due diligence required, the complexity and scope of the integration, cultural barriers to integration, and the potential for attrition among employees and customers. The good news, according to a 2015 McKinsey survey, is that companies that excel at post-merger integration deliver significantly higher returns to their shareholders than those that don't—returns 6–12 percentage points higher.[1]

Of course, seamlessly linking the strategic planning and analysis stage to the negotiation and integration phases is harder in practice than in theory, thanks to a host of challenges. For example: during the early stages of many deals (especially larger ones), senior executives often keep the M&A team small to ensure confidentiality. As the transaction progresses, however, it's usually advisable to increase the team's size to guarantee that enough expertise is deployed to properly value and negotiate the deal. As a transaction moves forward, it's also important that a "critical mass" of employees buy-in to the deal's rationale and be held accountable for achieving the anticipated synergies.

"But many M&A practitioners make the mistake of clinging to too small a team late into the due-diligence stages of a deal," reports McKinsey. "This overly conservative mind-set creates problems, leaving deal planners to perform

© The Author(s) 2019
N. Fernandes, *The Value Killers*, https://doi.org/10.1007/978-3-030-12216-4_3

their roles in isolation. Without others to challenge assumptions and cognitive biases, the planners' synergy estimates, performance benchmarks, and cost and revenue targets can be off the mark.... Business managers [later] complain that their synergy targets are too high – when in fact, they often prove to be too low. And companies lose precious time as those tasked with implementing a deal try to reconstruct the expectations of those who planned it."[2]

First Gulf Bank/Dubai First: Using the Same Team for Each Phase

Ideally, the acquiring company should assign the same team members to every phase of the transaction, including the integration.

This was the choice made by First Gulf Bank (FGB), the largest publicly traded bank in the United Arab Emirates, during its successful acquisition of Dubai First (DF), a financial player focused on consumer finance and credit cards. No sooner was FGB asked to submit a binding bid for the company than FGB's CFO Karim Karoui tapped Amit Talgeri, head of retail banking, to assemble an "A Team" from across the company's businesses and functions to evaluate the target and prepare a binding bid. "We wanted our first M&A to be very successful," said FGB's Karim Karoui. "We said, 'We cannot fail on our first M&A' ... so we invested in it – in terms of time, people, everything, to ensure that it worked. We took the best people. Everybody was excited about it; everybody was ready and motivated to play a big role. It was an A-team, without a doubt."

By enlisting about two dozen individuals to manage every stage of the transaction, FGB was able to readily identify the synergies in each team member's area of expertise. Moreover, because many team members went on to lead the integration effort—in some cases managing the newly acquired business units (at least temporarily)—FGB established clear accountability for achieving the synergy goals. The company empowered its people from end to end, creating direct and personal connections between every phase of the deal. "Besides synergies, one of the key success factors ... was that people had ownership of the project even before it closed," said Dubai First CEO Harish Krishnaswami. "Employees were empowered to make recommendations, and then were given the opportunity to implement them."

Even more important, FGB established a clear vision of how its existing product portfolio could be integrated with DF's portfolio to enhance revenues. In short, the acquiring company created a plan to link not only the transaction phases (before, during, and after), but for *how* to harness the anticipated synergies to transition the pre-merger companies to a new and more profitable post-deal organization.

In addition to leveraging DF's brand to sell FGB products to DF customers, the deal would provide opportunities for considerable economies of scale, given FGB's size and performance level. Having common systems, processes, and people could also contribute to cost savings. For example, the two stand-alone companies had a common card processor, but it was charging DF much higher rates than FGB (the latter was doing five times the amount of business with them). Operationally, both firms had strong sales teams that generated good business and steady revenues, but the sales operation at DF could be further streamlined and partially outsourced to realize additional cost savings.

(continued)

(continued)

Well before the deal was finalized, FGB team members "as experts in their respective areas of the business, were able to analyze each line item of DF's profit and loss statement in detail" and propose improvements and cost reductions that could be undertaken, said Naveed Pathan, FGB's head of strategy and financial control for consumer banking. "In the cards business, we were number one in the country, so we knew all the KPIs."

As a result, in part, of linking the before and after, FGB achieved overall performance improvements in record time, as well as a 275 percent year-on-year net profit growth. If it's not possible or desirable to deploy the same team members for every phase (e.g., because there simply isn't enough staff or the existing staff can't cope with the additional workload), a good alternative strategy is to ensure that the ultimate "owners" of the synergies become involved *before* the deal is closed.

Multiple Teams Can Produce Disappointing Results

All too often, acquiring companies create one internal team for the pre-deal analysis, a second (external) team to execute the deal, and a third team to manage the new acquisition. The typical buyer closes the deal and only *then* introduces a new team to oversee the integration—a team that has had nothing to do with the acquired firm until now.

As you can imagine, this frequently leads to disappointing results. When heretofore uninvolved managers are assigned the task of integrating new units, divisions, or an entire company, some will quickly conclude that they've been set up to fail. This is the unsurprising consequence of putting one group of people in charge of identifying synergies and performance goals and then leaving the "dirty work" to others. This is one reason why so many mergers fail.

(Note: some executives are *promoted* after spearheading bad deals. "I've seen people who were the driving forces behind deals, deals that went bad fairly quickly, emerge completely unhurt," said one of the executives interviewed. "That's just the reality of it. Some of these people acquired businesses that a few years later were shut down because they didn't deliver … and they got promoted into other roles.")

Failure to enlist the synergy owners during each phase reduces accountability. If a manager is tasked with achieving x, y, and z synergies, *that manager* should be rewarded for achieving the targets and punished for failure.

This was the strategy that InBev pursued following its acquisition of Anheuser-Busch in 2008—a strategy best summarized as "whether you make it or break it, you own the results." For example, as part of its "aggressive" approach to cost-cutting and cash management, InBev determined, shortly after the acquisition, that accounts payables to Anheuser-Busch suppliers would be extended to 120 days.

Did InBev CEO Carlos Brito simply wave his hand and announce, "Make it so?" Was that number plucked from a hat? Hardly. Instead, someone in Anheuser-Busch supply-chain management was asked to propose the largest time interval to which payables could be extended (without fomenting a supplier revolt). Once the number was offered, it was plugged into a spreadsheet, and right next to that 120-day figure was the name of the person who proposed it. That manager had now become responsible for achieving the 120-day target. If the goal was achieved, the manager received a big bonus. If the goal wasn't reached, negative consequences would ensue.

Though it may seem obvious that an M&A will create value only when the anticipated numbers actually materialize, and when those responsible for setting the performance goals are incentivized to achieve them, many companies don't take these "obvious" steps to accomplish the "obvious" objective of maximizing value creation.

Why Use Different Teams?

If it's advisable to link the before and after stages of an M&A by sending in a single team to manage the process, or by involving the synergy owners early, why do many companies continue to rotate different teams in and out of the transactions?

The executives and bankers interviewed for this book offered a variety of explanations, ranging from a desire to promote certain managers to higher positions in the newly merged entities to the belief that internal M&A teams should not lead integrations because the skill sets required to analyze and negotiate deals are different from those needed during the post-deal phase.

Other interviewees suggested that, for many companies, using different teams for different M&A phases was simply the standard approach to the division of labor during deals.

"This is how many companies are set up. They have an M&A team, which is very small (usually no more than 10 people) to help maintain confidentiality," said Marcus Hanana of P&G Europe. "They generally perform the due diligence, and when it's time to manage the integration, the company wants to involve a much larger share of the organization.... If it were my company, though, I would always get some senior executives and middle managers involved in the due diligence, because they will see things very differently from the M&A team. These middle managers will dive deeper, see organizational gaps faster and bring in the required business judgement about the quality of the teams and the underlying ability to integrate – all elements which pure data, analyzed from far, will fail to tell."

Another reason for different teams is to provide a check on biases. Stefan Koch of Dow Europe said, "I've been in negotiations in which a business representative is functioning as the sponsor – someone who really wants to do the deal. And the person starts getting red-faced when they think the legal team or the M&A team is killing the deal for them because we're asking questions or taking tough positions during negotiations."

On the other hand, added Koch, "the ultimate stakeholders should not be locked out as they will own the deal after implementation and naturally have deeper insight into the deal requirements for a successful future operation on the business."

In summary, business stakeholders have to be part of the deal team, even if they are hugely conflicted and biased. What's important is that you actively mitigate these biases by appointing someone to challenge the deal.

Wanted: Preparation and Follow-Through

Preparation is key to the success of any deal. Before entering negotiations, there is a lot of background preparation that can be done internally. The more you prepare ex ante, the fewer surprises will be left for the due-diligence period and the more focused the due diligence will be. Below are some pre-deal activities that can facilitate a more successful transaction:

- *Identify potential targets.* Develop and maintain up-to-date books for each potential target. Business units should appraise, on a periodic basis, this list of potential acquisitions, undertaking regular reviews of the strategic fit of each asset. These reviews should include, for each target:

  - *Growth potential:* markets, technologies, capacity, product launches.
  - *Cost savings:* technology, scale, capacity utilization.
  - *Other possible synergies and dis-synergies*, including customers, personnel, technology, and best practices.

- *Monitor investors and investor relations.* If the potential targets are publicly traded, keep track of their investor relations disclosures, analyst reports, forecasts, the names of the larger investors, any changes in the investor base over time, and so on.

- **Prepare answers to key questions.** For each potential target, develop straightforward answers to the questions "Why should we buy this company?, Where is the value coming from?, and What is our strategic intent if we *do* buy the company?"

- **Prepare a list of "deal team" members** who can spring into action the moment a deal is initiated. This should be a tangible list (not a few memorized names) of individuals representing departments and functions that include internal M&A, finance, marketing, operations, legal, and so on. The team should be ready to manage the transaction from A to Z.

- **External resources.** In addition, prepare and routinely update a database of external advisers to complement your internal resources. It's important to move fast once the deal period arrives, so the list of contacts (law firms, investment banks, auditors, etc.) should be assembled well in advance.

- **Integration planning.** This type of planning must be done as early as possible, and should encompass processes, documentation, identification of key staff and customers (and how to work with them), system infrastructure, operational issues, and so on. By the closing, the plan should also contain detailed communication strategies and tactics to help prevent a mass exodus of customers and talented employees. (One interviewee suggested that this planning take place during the period when anti-trust officials are examining the deal.)

- **In a divestiture scenario**, preparation should include intellectual property issues, branding, systems, legal entities, identification of shared facilities/centers, long-term off-take agreements, and market pricing, as well as an assessment of what would be needed to run the business on a stand-alone basis. In addition, a large volume of documents and other data can be assembled for access in a virtual data room (VDR). Preparing and organizing information, from income statements and balance sheets to cash flow statements, requires a substantial amount of time (and expense), so it's a good idea to launch the preparations far in advance. (It's common to prepare three years' worth of historical data and two to three years of forecasts, but this can vary widely from deal to deal.)

Needless to say, estimates prepared during the pre-deal phase must be thoroughly followed through during the post-merger period. If the pre-deal estimates are used to justify a certain valuation, then, in the post-merger period, those numbers must materialize for the deal to create value for the shareholders.

The FGB/DF acquisition and the InBev-Anheuser-Bush merger (see pages 18 and 32 for case study) are prime examples of transactions based on well-integrated processes that linked the three M&A phases. In both cases, the acquirers established clear accountability for achieving anticipated synergies by attaching someone's name to every number that was plugged into the valuation. In both cases, there was a clear understanding of *who* would be "the owner" of each line of synergies and where and how the synergies would be realized.

After the InBev/Anheuser-Busch merger, for example, the acquirer retained a significant percentage of the target's staff to help them achieve the major cost-cutting benefits. To ensure the Anheuser-Busch staff was properly motivated, InBev identified 40 executives of Anheuser-Busch that they believed were key to a successful integration, promising them $1.3 billion in stock options if the company managed to reduce its debt to "normal levels" within five years of the acquisition. In the end, the goal of reducing the net debt to core EBITDA ratio (from 5.5 at the time of the purchase to 2.5) was achieved in just three years, triggering the big bonuses for the AB executives.[3]

Contrast this success with the problems that ensued when a large consumer products company failed to link the before and after stages of their acquisition. (This case is also a cautionary tale about underestimating the impact of cultural differences.)

Here, the seller manufactured a well-known product that was sold in retail outlets (e.g., supermarkets and drugstores) and the salons of "beauty" professionals. According to a source familiar with the deal, the acquisition was part of the buyer's long-term strategy of adding large, popular brands to its growing family of products to achieve cost and revenue synergies. In this case, however, it appears that either (a) the deal's rationale was never properly aligned with the integration planning or (b) the people responsible for identifying the biggest sources of value failed to coordinate their efforts with those responsible for the integration.

The [acquired company] followed a business model we knew nothing about. The initial business model was built on a type of refill model: The company would finance the furniture and equipment of a newly opened coiffeur/beauty salons and in return, the owner contracts on the professional salon brand for a certain period of time, generally 5-10 years…. We had little clue how to do that: how to manage and organize around that model, or how to talk to these [professionals]. So what happened? The business, whilst growing before – stalled and contracted because the people who knew how the business worked…they left… and now we had a business that we didn't know how to manage as it wasn't part of our core strength which was growing big, global brands and drive them via retail. We eventually sold the business after many years, but while we owned it, sales went down by double digit percentages. It was a painful experience.

Culture: The Universal Scapegoat

When seemingly good M&As "unexpectedly" go bad, one of the most common explanations given by CEOs is that the organizations' cultures turned out to be a mismatch. In many instances, however, "culture" is merely a convenient scapegoat. All too often, culture is the "Go-To" excuse that boards and senior management use to mask other explanations for the deal's failure—explanations that might lay blame at their own feet. (*Note*: For the purposes of this book, I define *culture* as simply "the way we do things around here.")

I'm not suggesting that cultural differences are never (or only rarely) the cause of problematic integrations. Far from it. Cultural alignment is one of many critical success factors in any value-creating transaction. What I *am* suggesting is that culture is a poor choice as a universal scapegoat because there are many ways for internal and external M&A teams to identify, diagnose, and prevent synergy-killing culture clashes at various stages of the process. Executives who default to "cultural mismatch" justifications are basically asking employees, customers, and investors to believe that there was no way they could have anticipated cultural problems. They are asking to be viewed like the unlucky farmer whose wheat field was just washed away by a rogue thunderstorm. (Who could have predicted *that*, right?)

Unfortunately, an alarmingly high percentage of acquiring companies put themselves in the position of the poor farmer. According to one survey, most organizations "have not yet developed a structured process to effectively diagnose, manage and integrate organizational culture – even in light of the fact that almost 75 percent regard culture as a key component in creating deal value."[4]

Another study reported that, though companies cite cultural integration issues as one of the top two causes of deal failure, 58 percent said they did not have a specific approach to assessing and integrating culture in a deal. Of the firms that lost key talent at higher-than-normal rates during transactions, 68 percent did not have a specific approach for culture.

Most disturbing, none (0 percent) of the surveyed companies reported that its cultural integration practices were effective. In addition, over 50 percent of companies reported that they had failed to achieve their stated objectives in past transactions, and over 50 percent stated that they had lost key talent at the same rate—or a higher rate—than non-critical talent.[5]

In sum, too few companies analyze the cultural compatibility of the targets prior to the deal, even though most executives recognize the dangers of ignoring this issue. When cultural considerations are left out of the process, the consequences can include plummeting employee productivity, high rates of worker and customer attrition, delayed and canceled orders, and so on.

If we further define culture as the shared values that drive the behaviors of employees to desired outcomes, then the Chrysler/Daimler-Benz merger of 1998 is probably the best—or at least the most infamous—example of a culture clash that led to "epic failure."

When Cultures Collide: The Daimler-Chrysler Debacle

When German automaker Daimler-Benz and American auto manufacturer Chrysler merged in a $36 billion deal, it was billed as a "merger of equals." It soon became apparent, however, that (a) it would be Daimler executives who called the shots and (b) there was little or no cultural fit between the organizations. While Chrysler's culture was frequently described as "creative," "open," and "freewheeling," Daimler practiced a more traditional command-and-control style of management—one often characterized as "conservative" or "safe."

Although the deal's rationale was sound (it was based on synergies that were expected to accrue from technology and resource sharing), the operations and management of the companies were never able to properly integrate because of their radically different approaches to many issues. Without this integration, no synergies could be achieved.

In addition to differences in management style, the chief cultural difference between the two companies was their respective attitudes toward serving customers. While Daimler valued reliability and achieving the highest levels of quality, Chrysler prized appealing designs and competitive prices. This resulted in conflicting orders and goals among different departments, which tended to move in opposite directions.

Just as important was the issue of trust. Employees at both firms were reluctant to work with one another, particularly on the Chrysler side. During the early stages of integration, large numbers of key Chrysler executives resigned or were replaced by their German counterparts. Hence, a significant number of Chrysler employees became convinced that the so-called merger of equals was in reality a hostile takeover of their corporate culture.[6]

In the merger's first year, Daimler-Chrysler delivered $1 billion in savings by combining purchasing and back-office functions. But following these quick victories, there were significant coordination problems between Daimler and Chrysler, including a complete lack of post-merger synergy in engineering and research and development. Worse, large numbers of Chrysler executives and engineers began fleeing the combined entity after the Germans attempted to "bulldoze" Chrysler's culture in favor of their own.

Nine years later, Daimler called it quits and sold the American brand for just $9 billion.

(continued)

(continued)

It's not often that observers are able to isolate a single, overriding cause for the failure of an M&A, but in the case of Daimler-Chrysler, there is a near-universal consensus that the destruction of more than $30 billion in value was the result of profound culture differences. The culture clash between the two organizations led to massive breakdowns in coordination and a severe lack of trust among the employees. In turn, this spawned frequent communication failures that contributed to a sharp reduction in productivity. Collectively, these factors led to the downfall of a combined company that—at least on paper—once had a very promising future.

Insights from Successful Culture Warriors

Culture collisions rarely rise to the level of Daimler-Chrysler, but most companies make some of the same mistakes. Chief among them is adopting a "one-size-fits-all" approach to cultural integration.

"Don't assume you should always use a standardized handbook to guide your integration," said transition CEO Huibert Vigeveno, discussing the integration of BG Group into the Shell Group. "What might have worked for an M&A transaction ten years ago won't necessarily work today."[7]

During my interview with Vigeveno, he added, "What a lot of companies also do … particularly the company acquiring … is [exhibit] an alpha male behavior. 'We're acquiring you, so let us tell you what we want and how we want it. My view was, 'We're paying a significant premium, and you [BG] are known as the most agile company in the oil and gas industry. So let's really work together to make this a world-class integration … and to a springboard for change in Shell, not only to integrate BG.' And the best way to do that was to work together as one team with one mindset."

Dow Europe's Koch agreed that "no single recipe works in every situation. Sometimes, on the integration side, the best thing is to apply the acquirer's work processes and best practices quickly. We have had acquisitions where we wanted to keep them independent for as long as possible. That can be a valid strategy, but it comes with a cost. It comes at the cost of delaying the implementation of certain synergies and efficiencies. And it comes at the risk that the target doesn't learn as fast as it could – that you don't synergize most of the knowledge."

[Y]ou have to have general strategy – long leash, short leash, that's all fine – but then you have to challenge yourself and change your approach … based on what you discover about the target.

Several of the executives interviewed stressed the need for strong leadership throughout the integration. "I think you really need to have a strong management team who is handling this, with as much support as possible, and getting the job done as quickly as possible," said Casper Kirketerp-Moeller of Clever A/S.

Should Culture Ever Be a Deal Killer?

Can the cultures of two companies be so incompatible that no amount of integration will work, and the parties should walk away? Or is effective cultural integration merely a matter of adequately preparing for these differences to ensure that they are quickly and tactfully managed?

I posed this question to all of the experts interviewed. Although opinions varied, the majority believe that while cultural incompatibility *could* be a deal killer, the dangers should be identified and assessed long before there's any deal to be killed. That being said, several interviewees indicated that certain types of M&As pose greater risks than others. In these cases, even higher attention should be given to cultural due diligence. These are some examples of the M&A types that require strong care to the cultural dimensions.

When the Target Is a Family-Owned Business "If you have a very strong family-run company that is changing hands to an ownership structure that is completely different, that is very, very complicated," said Halbart Völker of NIBC Bank NV. "You have to deal with a large number of people who have been with the company for 10, 20 or 30 years. They have all worked for the owner of the company, who was personally involved in running the business. They are extremely loyal to the seller, so to step in as the new owner … is very challenging. There are, of course, stories of family-owned businesses that changed hands and became more successful, but in general it's a very challenging experience."

When Customers Are Loyal to the Target's Way of Doing Things Following his firm's acquisition of a smaller company in the same industry, said one interviewee, "we failed to understand the difference in their way of serving customers versus ours. When we integrated the company into our structure, the [target lost the ability] to serve customers in the ways they were used to. Our thinking was … Okay, our website is much better, our app is much better, the product offering is much better, both in range and depth. There's also much more support; you can get many more services. You should be a happy customer! But apparently, there were customers who had other preferences that we had ignored… So we lost revenue of 10 to 14 million euros. So I would say it was a perfect operation, but the patient almost died."

Cross-Border Deals in Which the Acquirer Is Dominated by a Single Nationality Said one interviewee about a European auto manufacturer (not Daimler-Benz), "Take ABC company, for example. Do you think that's an international company? I don't think so. Show me one foreigner on the board or at the C-Suite level. Even at the C-Suite-minus-one level, you won't find any non-[nationality] members. That's not an international company. That's a [nation]-based company that is internationally successful. Yes, they have salespeople in the U.S., but the head of development is not American. Guess what nationality he is? When people have a hard time even communicating in a different language, how well do you think the different cultures will mesh?"

Culture Integration Solutions

Does culture impact later performance? Yes, there is a positive correlation between cultural *awareness* and the success of deals after the close. This doesn't mean, however, that acquirers should only pursue targets with similar cultures. It *does* mean that buyers must be aware, during the pre-deal phase, of the cultures, and take this into account when preparing for integration.

During a well-managed M&A, the majority of cultural issues will be identified—and solutions prepared—before the deal closes. According to the model developed by Dr. Daniel Denison, currently Professor of Organization Development at IMD, the core challenges to be addressed are beliefs, assumptions, and their associated behaviors, with success occurring when all three factors are combined to foster outcomes that create value rather than destroying it. The Denison model allows organizations to uncover the underlying beliefs and assumptions in recognizable and measurable ways that impact organizational performance. Specifically, the model answers four key questions about an organization[8]:

1. **Mission: Do you know where you are going?** Do employees understand the strategies of the organization, and do they think the strategies will work? Are there short-term goals that help link what employees do on a day-to-day basis to the company's strategy and vision? Do employees

understand how their jobs fit in? Most important, do employees share a common vision for the company, and does this vision motivate and excite them?

2. **Adaptability: Are you listening to the marketplace?** Can employees read the external environment and react to trends and changes? Do they constantly look for new and improved ways to do their jobs? Does the company understand the needs of its customers, and are employees committed to responding to the changing needs of customers? Is importance placed on learning in the workplace? Does the company create an environment in which reasonable risk-taking and innovation can occur? Is knowledge shared across the entire organization?

3. **Involvement: Are your people aligned, engaged, and capable?** Do employees feel informed and involved in the work they do? Do they feel they can have a positive impact on the organization? Is teamwork encouraged *and* practiced throughout the company? Further, do employees believe that they are being invested in, and that their skills are improving? Does the organization have the skills it needs to compete today and tomorrow?

4. **Consistency. Do you have the values, systems, and processes in place to execute?** Do employees share a set of core values that create a strong sense of identity and a clear set of expectations? Do leaders model and reinforce these values? Is the organization able to reach agreement on critical issues? Can employees reconcile differences in a constructive way when problems arise? Do employees from different parts of the organization share a common perspective that allows them to work effectively across organizational boundaries? Do they work to eliminate silos and promote actions that serve the best interests of the company as a whole?

The optimum time to investigate the culture of the target, so that key similarities and differences between the companies can be identified, is during due diligence—after the target has been identified and the M&A teams have begun sharing financial and legal information. It is also "important to consider the expected degree of integration that the merger or acquisition will require. Will it be a holding company that is allowed a great deal of operating independence and thus less intensive cultural integration? Is it being absorbed into the acquiring firm in a way that will require significant change for the acquired firm? Which parts of the acquiring organization will be most influenced by the acquisition?"[9]

The due-diligence period also provides acquirers with an ideal opportunity to gauge the target's culture via interviews and routine interactions with their management. The acquirer's management and M&A team members can also exploit informal occasions—for example, lunches and dinners—to learn more about the seller from the people who work there.

Such techniques are heartily endorsed by Anastasia Kovaleva of Bain & Company. She said it's important that people from both companies meet before the deal, and not just in a negotiating environment. "In negotiations and management meetings, it's all about presenting ... with questions going back and forth and due diligence. But having people connect on a different level – in an informal environment – is actually quite valuable. People get to see each other in a more normal environment" and will talk "about how they would run the business. And not just on paper ... but thinking through what the strategy could be going forward for the company."

In the case of a cross-border M&A, another factor to consider when assessing the cultural "fit" is the acquiring firm's and the target's track record with such transactions. Previous experience with foreign deals, including JVs and strategic partnerships, has been shown to increase the success of later cross-border mergers and acquisitions.[10]

Because not all culture data is accessible during the early stages of due diligence, it is recommended that the acquiring company collect different types of data before the M&A is announced:

- **Social media data, comments, forums, including the company reply to complaints.**
- Data from employer review sites (such as Glassdoor and Indeed), which contain millions of company reviews, CEO approval ratings, salary reports, interview reviews and questions, benefits reviews, and so on.
- **Interviews with** former executives and employees for their insights into the target company and its culture.
- **External stakeholder interviews with** customers, vendors, channel partners, and other external stakeholders that interact with the company.

After the merger or acquisition is announced, Denison recommends that the acquirer conduct:

- **HR data and document reviews:** Use existing HR data and documents (e.g., employee surveys) to gain insight into the target company's culture. Ninety-six percent of Fortune 500 companies administer employee surveys with relevant culture questions.

- **Internal stakeholder interviews:** Speak with the target firm's leadership team, a sample of the middle managers, and a sample of front-line employees.[11]

Don't overlook the value of employee incentive schemes (like the $1.3 billion bonus program InBev developed for Anheuser-Busch executives) to prod culture in the right direction. Prior to the merger, the cultures of these two companies could not have been less alike. While InBev ruthlessly focused on cost-cutting, lean offices, and economy-class travel (a no-frills culture if ever there was one), the target company, Anheuser-Busch, had a lavish corporate culture exemplified by its fleet of private jets and generous fringe benefits for employees. The InBev incentive program not only helped the company to promote cultural buy-in among executives who were otherwise shell-shocked by the latter's heavy-handed approach to integration (e.g., InBev immediately destroyed AB's "spendthrift" culture), but also provided them with a *lot* of motivation to exceed InBev's ambitious (some would say "draconian") cost-cutting goals. (See case study on page 18.)

Another proven way of promoting a smoother cultural integration is to openly debate it together. In my executive training and consulting experience, we often conduct intensive executive workshops for the post-merged entities, to encourage executives of the two companies to identify cultural commonalities and differences, design preferred end states, and brainstorm creative approaches to achieve the end states (see also the section on Synergy Summits in Chap. 4).

Of course, culture cannot be changed in a vacuum. Other organizational design elements, including processes and structure, need to change. One cannot hope to simply combine two disparate cultures and hope for the best. Management needs to develop an organizational framework to help guide the design of the new culture.

One such framework is known as "the Star Model." Developed by Jay R. Galbraith, this framework for organization design serves as a foundation on which a company can base its design choices. The framework consists of a series of design policies that are controllable by management and can influence employee behavior. The policies are the tools with which management must become skilled in order to shape the decisions and behaviors of their organizations effectively.

In the Star Model, design policies fall into five categories. The first is strategy, which determines direction. The second is structure, which determines the location of decision-making power. The third is processes, which have to do with the flow of information. The fourth is rewards and reward systems, which influence the motivation of people to perform and address organizational goals. The fifth is made up of policies relating to people (human resource policies), which influence and frequently define the employees' mind-sets and skills.[12] Successful companies are those that have a strong alignment across these five categories. But the recommended implementation of its five individual components depends substantially on the desired end state that is desired for the merged entity.

Desired End State

From the very beginning, the M&A team of the acquirer should understand—and plan for—a desired cultural "end state." Again, there is no one-size-fits-all solution to cultural integration. Instead, there exists a continuum that ranges from "Bulldozing through" the seller's culture to "Leaving them alone."

Bulldozing Through   Leaving Them Alone

←————————————————————————————————————→

"Bulldozing through" means that the target company embraces the culture of the acquirer. And its structures, processes, incentive systems, and so on will be implemented in the acquired company.

"Leaving them alone" implies that the acquired company is left untouched—that is, both companies retain separate and distinct cultures. And we can thus sustain different ways of working in the two different companies.

Between these extremes lie an almost infinite number of possibilities, challenges, and choices that—from the very outset—must be met with adequate preparation and planning.

The "right choice" depends on the purpose of the M&A and where the value is coming from. If the value of the deal lies in cost-cutting, then the standards of costs, operations, efficiency, and so on of the acquirer will be imposed on the target (assuming the acquirer has better costs). If the deal's value rests with the skills and expertise of the target's personnel—as is often the case with disruptive IT companies—the astute buyer should do their best to ensure that this valuable asset remains happy and productive.

Whichever solution is chosen, a successful integration can be achieved only if both organizations develop a clear and shared understanding of the ultimate goal—a goal that must be identified upfront as part of the cultural due diligence. After identifying the differences, any measures of cultural integration should be clearly linked to the sources of the deal's value creation.

Summary

It is vital that companies establish a well-integrated, continuous process linking the pre-deal phase, the deal period, and the post-deal phase. This is a crucial feature of successful deals. Ideally, companies should assign the same team members to every phase of the transaction, including the post-merger integration. If this isn't possible (e.g., because there isn't sufficient staff and/or existing staff can't manage the additional workload), it is critical that the "owners of the synergies" be involved *before* the deal is closed.

Too often, companies create an internal team for the pre-deal analysis; a second (external) team to execute the deal, and a third team to manage the new acquisition. Tapping heretofore uninvolved managers to lead the new organization or business units is a common mistake. Failure to use "synergy owners" during each phase eliminates accountability. If a manager is tasked with achieving x, y, and z synergies, that manager should be rewarded for achieving the targets and punished for failure.

Estimates during the pre-deal phase must be thoroughly followed through in the post-merger period. If pre-deal estimates are used to justify a certain valuation, then, in the post-merger period, it is necessary that those numbers actually materialize for the deal to create value for shareholders.

Preparation is important. Before entering the deal period, there is a lot of background preparation that can be done internally. The more you prepare ex ante, the fewer surprises are left for due diligence, and the more focused is that due diligence.

The InBev-AB merger is a prime example of a well-integrated process that linked the three phases, despite the two companies having originally very different cultures. This deal featured:

- Clear accountability. Each number plugged into the valuation had a name attached to it. This allowed them to clearly identify the synergies (in each member's area of expertise).
- Clear understanding of where, how, and *who* would be responsible for each line of synergies.
- "The best of both worlds." InBev retained some top AB staff to help achieve major benefits.

Although executives frequently cite "culture" to mask other failure reasons, the importance of cultural alignment should not be underestimated. Few companies analyze the compatibility of the businesses beforehand, while more than half don't prioritize a review of leadership capability within the two organizations. Ignoring the collaboration requirements of an M&A at each step can be a fast track to failure. When cultural considerations are left out of the mix, a host of critical problems can result, including plummeting employee productivity and attrition, delayed/canceled customer orders, and so on. The Chrysler/Daimler-Benz merger is a cautionary tale of the danger of an acquirer forcing its own culture on a seller.

Other cultural integration mistakes include adopting a one-size-fits-all approach; having a pre-defined expectation of how cultures will merge; not knowing when to bulldoze the target's culture and when to leave it alone; and a lack of strong leadership. Key cultural challenges to address (per the Denison model) are mission, adaptability, involvement, and consistency.

Should culture ever be a deal killer? At well-run companies, the majority of cultural issues will be identified—and solutions prepared—before the deal. There is a continuum of options—from "Bulldozing" to "Leave them alone." Many possibilities are available, and the "right one" depends on the M&A's purpose and the sources of its value.

Does culture impact M&A performance later on? Yes, there is a positive correlation between cultural *awareness* and the success of deals. However, this doesn't mean that acquirers should only pursue targets with similar cultures. It *does* mean that buyers must be aware, during the pre-deal phase, of the two corporate cultures, and take this into account when preparing integration plans (as in the InBev-AB case). Pre-deal preparation is key, including interviews with former employees of the target to better understand cultural differences and their relevance; social media data analysis; and incentives schemes like the one deployed by InBev.

Ultimately, culture cannot be changed in a vacuum. Other organizational design elements, including processes, rewards, and structure, need to change. Management needs to develop an organizational framework to help guide design of the new culture.

Questions for Future M&As

- Does your company change the composition of the team during the process?
- Does your company typically nominate a new person (not involved in the negotiation, pre-deal, due diligence, etc.) to run the combined company (or acquired entity)?
- Does your company keep members of the initial deal team (pre-deal analysis) involved in the last phase—Integration?

- Are synergies attributable to a specific person (or group of people)?
- Is there an incentive scheme for achieving proposed synergies? What about penalties if these are not achieved?
- Does your organization maintain an updated list of prospective Deal Team members—individuals from the internal M&A department, finance, marketing, operations, legal, and so on?
- Does your organization ever conduct external stakeholders' interviews, social media data analysis, synergy workshops, or encourage informal interactions with members of the other organizations' management/M&A team?
- Does your company make use of any incentive programs to encourage the target's management and employees to meet major M&A goals and objectives?
- Does your company keep updated, on a regular basis, lists of potential targets, along with answers to key questions about each target?
- Does your company have a specific approach to cultural issues?

Notes

1. Rebecca Doherty, Oliver Engert, and Andy West, "How the best acquirers excel at integration," McKinsey & Company, January 2016.
2. Jeff Rudnicki, Ryan Thorpe, and Andy West, "The artful synergist, or how to get more value from mergers and acquisitions." McKinsey & Company, February 2017.
3. John Weeks, "AB INBEV: Dream, People, Culture and Cost." IMD case study, 2015.
4. "The impact of culture on M&A." Mercer Ltd., 2009.
5. "Culture Integration in M&A: Survey Findings." Aon Hewitt, 2011.
6. http://www.commisceo-global.com/blog/cultural-differences-in-international-merger-and-acquisitions#C1
7. "Delivering a world-class integration in oil & gas," McKinsey & Company, February 2017.
8. "Getting Started with Your Denison Organizational Survey Results," Denison Consulting, 2009.
9. Daniel R. Denison, Bryan Adkins and Ashley M. Guidroz, "Managing Cultural Integration in Cross-Border Mergers and Acquisitions." Advances in Global Leadership. Emerald Group Publishing Limited, 2011.
10. Ibid.
11. www.denisonconsulting.com/cultural-due-diligence-helping-mergers-and-acquisitions-succeed/
12. http://www.jaygalbraith.com/images/pdfs/StarModel.pdf

4

Think Like a Financial Investor

One of my favorite movie characters is Gordon Gekko, the investor and corporate raider who first appeared in the 1987 film *Wall Street*. Though Gekko has become a cultural symbol for greed and corruption, as epitomized by his famous "greed is good" speech, the fictional takeover specialist has some redeeming qualities that M&A teams would be wise to emulate. Among other things, Gekko was clearheaded, dispassionate, and single-minded in the pursuit of profit, his dedication to maximizing shareholder value, and his choice of acquisition targets.

Everyone remembers the line "greed … is good," but many forget that before saying this, Gekko chastised Teldar Paper's management in front of the shareholders for their lavish compensation packages and small ownership stake, and boasted about his own commitment to value creation:

> All together, these men … own less than three percent of the company…. You own the company. That's right, you, the stockholder. And you are all being royally screwed over by these … bureaucrats, with their luncheons, their hunting and fishing trips, their corporate jets and golden parachutes…. In the last seven deals that I've been involved with, there were 2.5 million stockholders who have made a pretax profit of 12 billion dollars.

More important (but less famously) was Gekko's advice to never get emotional about investments. Given the high stakes involved in many mergers and acquisitions, however, this advice can be challenging to implement. With huge sums riding on deal outcomes, as well as careers, egos, promotions, and the long-term futures of the companies, M&As can be emotion-packed odysseys during which management can lose sight of reality.

© The Author(s) 2019
N. Fernandes, *The Value Killers*, https://doi.org/10.1007/978-3-030-12216-4_4

Too often, instead of retaining the viewpoint of disinterested, third-party financial investors, deal participants get caught up in the drama. This increases the odds that the transaction will generate more and more momentum until it assumes a life of its own. This, in turn, increases the odds that the "sunk cost fallacy" will kick in—that is, that instead of making decisions based on anticipated synergies and value creation, decisions will become clouded by the "emotional investments" of the participants. They may come to believe that they have traveled too far to abandon the deal now.

"I call it being a hostage of the process," said Michael Jeppesen of Solar A/S Group. "You start to see all the advantages and start to convince yourself that the risks can be managed … that it's all under control… We're clearly going to get something we don't like and we know it's going to cause problems based on the experiences we have had, but still we continue down that road."

Most Acquirers Overpay

Even when dealmakers lose sight of the original rationale and objectives, financial markets never do. When M&As are announced, the markets do an uncanny (and merciless) job of predicting the long-term consequences. And in most cases, the markets punish the shareholders of the acquirer and reward those of the target.

Over many decades, studies of the value created by M&As for the bidder and target companies have uncovered overwhelming evidence suggesting that most merger gains are passed to the target's shareholders through the premium paid, which averages 25–30 percent. These studies typically found negative returns for the acquiring companies during the period around the announcement, which can be interpreted as value destruction.[1] Several studies also analyzed long-term returns to shareholders of the acquiring companies and tended to find negative returns to the acquirers.[2]

Obviously, due to the premium offered, the target's stockholders gain a substantial amount in the days after the acquisition announcement. It's interesting to note, however, that when the cumulative market value of the target and the acquiring firms is calculated—just before and just after the announcement—the average value *increases*. What this suggests is that the markets *do* see value added from synergies or other sources in a typical merger, but they also believe the acquiring firms are overestimating the value of the synergies and paying too much.[3] That is, most mergers make sense, and there is value being created. But acquirers tend to pay too much and pass thus along all the benefits to the seller shareholders.

What Would Gordon Gekko Do?

When it comes to negotiating value-creating M&As, it pays to think like a financial investor. As a rule, financial investors do better deals than their corporate/industrial counterparts. So before considering a deal, you may want to ask yourself "What would Gordon Gekko do in this situation?"

Or, if you prefer not to think like a movie villain, you could ask, "What would Warren Buffett do?" In a CNBC interview[4] during which he was asked about his valuation metrics for banks, Buffet responded: "[My valuation] metric was handed down by Aesop in 600 and something B.C., which is really the future cash compared to the present cash – the cash you have to lay out now and the cash you expect to get back later. And Aesop said that a bird in the hand is worth two in the bush. He didn't know what discount rate to use and the certainty of those two being in the bush, but a bank is no different than any other business. It's how much cash you're going to get between now and judgement day, discounted and compared to other investments."

Buffet and other successful investors employ sound financial models to determine if deals are worth pursuing—models such as discounted cash flow (DCF), market multiples, transaction multiples, and previous premiums paid. Most importantly, as opposed to many corporate buyers, they are cold-blooded. Deals are done when value is created, and they tend to not get emotional about deals. They exercise the discipline to say "no" when the numbers don't add up; they avoid bidding wars and—most important—they do NOT fall in love with the deals. This means that financial investors know when to walk away, which is no easy task. In contrast, in most companies, nobody is congratulated for abandoning a deal after the M&A teams have slaved over them for months, even when terminating the deal is the most sensible course.

"It's critical that you don't say yes to all the deals – that you eventually stop if you see that it's going beyond the point where value is created," said Sandeep Jalan of Aperam. "But there is also the human side of it, which is normal, that there will be disappointment. People pat you on the back if you close the deal: 'Great! We closed that deal.' No one pats you on the back to say, 'Congratulations, you did *not* close the deal.'"

The executives in charge of the deal must stay in control their emotions. Overconfidence, ego, and the sunk cost fallacy can lead otherwise intelligent people down the path to value destruction.

In addition to emotions, empirical research suggests that the amount of value created or destroyed by an M&A depends on a number of other factors,[5] including:

- **Company size:** Larger companies typically make worse deals. Bidder announcement returns are negatively related to company size.
- **Leverage:** Leveraged companies typically make better deals. Bidder announcement returns are positively correlated to the bidder's pre-acquisition leverage.
- **Diversification:** Mergers that focus on the company's core activity are more likely to enhance stockholder value, whereas diversifying mergers typically destroy value.
- **Deal size:** When the deal size is large relative to the acquirer's size, returns tend to be negative.
- **Payment method:** Stock-for-stock exchanges tend to generate lower returns for the buyer. Paying with stock seems cheaper, as no cash leaves the company's accounts. However, this turns out to lead to poorer deals, with bigger overpayment.
- **Cash flow level:** Cash-rich companies make worse deals. High levels of free cash flow induce empire-building acquisitions, and there is an empirical negative relationship between bidder returns and the cash-flows-to-equity ratio.
- **Whether the company is public or private.** Private companies make better deals, with higher synergies captured, than publicly traded companies.
- **Cultural differences:** Greater cultural differences between the countries of origin of the companies are associated with poorer-performing M&As.

As many as two-thirds of acquirers fail to achieve the benefits planned at the outset of the acquisition—a statistic that may be due to the fact that many buyers are more concerned about top-line growth than value creation. Other acquirers are so fixated on the numbers that they overlook the needs, desires, and sensitivities of the employees and customers that are being acquired.[6]

Telefónica-Vivo: The Price Was Not Right

In 2010, Telefónica was the third largest telephone company in the world by number of subscribers,[7] behind China Mobile and Vodafone. The company had been present in Brazil since 1996 when it acquired CRT, a fixed-line and mobile operator serving the southern part of the country. In 2003, Telefónica entered a 50/50 partnership with Portugal Telecom (PT) to acquire a 60 percent interest in Vivo, Brazil's leading mobile operator, which subsequently experienced double-digit annual growth.

Thanks to its stake in Vivo, as well as CRT and Telesp (which provided fixed wire line and broadband communications in São Paulo), Brazil became the largest contributor to Telefónica's revenues outside of Spain, accounting for 15 percent of the total. And with Spain facing tough economic times, growth in revenues or EBITDA was coming only from Latin America.

(continued)

(continued)

In 2010, Telefónica made three bids for PT's share of the joint venture. The first bid of €5.7 billion, tendered on May 10, represented a premium of 100 percent of Vivo's market value. Telefónica's leaders hoped to merge Vivo with Telesp, believing the deal would better prepare that company for the future. Because the two businesses had overlapping operations, staff, and systems, Telefónica expected to realize average synergies of €2.8 billion. However, it would take three or four years to fully exploit the synergies before they translated into an anticipated revenue increase of 1 percent for the combined companies.

Although Telefónica maintained that PT's shareholders would benefit the most from the deal, PT's management consistently responded to the bids by indicating that its stake in Vivo was not for sale, and that Vivo's value to Telefónica was much higher than the Spanish company's offer reflected. At one point, PT chief executive Zeinal Bava even stated that selling its Brazilian asset would "amputate PT's future." Unsurprisingly, PT's board unanimously rejected the first offer on the grounds that divesting Vivo would be detrimental to PT's long-term growth.

Telefónica soon followed up with a second offer of €6.5 billion, which was again rejected by PT's board as too stingy. Undeterred, Telefónica raised the price again on June 29—this time to €7.5 billion. At a meeting the next day, 74 percent of PT shareholders accepted the bid.

Was this a case of irrational exuberance—of a buyer that allowed a deal to acquire "runaway momentum?" The final price of the acquisition was more than the entire market capitalization of the PT group before the bid, and it proved a very expensive move for Telefónica, which had to finance the purchase by issuing additional debt. This caused its credit rating to be downgraded (to just above junk status) and forced the company to suspend dividends. Ultimately, Telefónica cornered itself into a value destroying solution, killed other strategic options in the process, and suffered from strong overconfidence from some of its top executives.

Syngenta Rejects Tempting Bids from Monsanto

Five years after Telefónica's acquisition of Vivo, the Swiss agrichemicals giant Syngenta rejected several tempting offers from Monsanto, the St. Louis-based company best known for its genetically engineered crop strains.

Like Telefónica, Monsanto made several takeover bids for the target company, each time raising the price (and the number of concessions it was willing to make) until the final offer reached an impressive $47 billion. Like PT, a majority of Syngenta's shareholders favored the final offer.[8] But unlike PT's management, Syngenta's leaders held steadfast to their belief that the price significantly undervalued the company and that the deal was "fraught with execution risk." (Among other concerns, Syngenta worried that the transaction would be derailed by any number of legal and regulatory issues, though Monsanto expressed confidence that such hurdles could be overcome.)

(continued)

(continued)

Ironically, an earlier Monsanto bid of $45 billion would have valued Syngenta at about 17 times earnings before interest, taxes, depreciation, and amortization in the previous 12 months. By comparison, large agrichemical transactions during the previous decade commanded a median multiple of about 12 times. This means that the purchase of Syngenta would have ranked as one of the industry's most costly deals to date. Had the deal closed, it also would have been the biggest ever acquisition of a European company by a U.S. rival.[9]

In this case, however, fortune—and the financial markets—favored the not so bold. Immediately after the collapse of the deal, shares of Monsanto rose by 8 percent, reflecting investors' relief that the company's increasingly expensive pursuit was finally over. Although shares of Syngenta fell significantly the day of the announcement, they quickly recovered.

Ironically, barely six months after Syngenta rejected the $47 billion takeover bid by Monsanto, the China National Chemical Corporation (a.k.a. "ChemChina") acquired it for "just" $43 billion.

Ultrapar-Ipiranga: The Right Deal at the Right Time

From 2001 to 2007, improving economic conditions in Brazil facilitated strong growth in the oil sector. It was a climate well suited to mergers and acquisitions for companies willing to act quickly and decisively. At first glance, therefore, the decision by Brazilian conglomerate Ultrapar to spearhead the acquisition of Grupo Ipiranga (Brazil's second-largest fuel distributor) might seem a little incongruous.

In terms of financial policy, Ultrapar was a conservative player with a strong focus on cash generation. Its principal corporate goals were to enhance shareholder value and strengthen its market presence by growing its businesses. For seven years following its 1999 IPO, it delivered total shareholder returns of 400 percent (an average annual return of 24 percent), and its profits grew from BRL 88 million to BRL 282 million. Ultrapar operated through three 100-percent-owned subsidiaries: (1) Oxiteno, the largest producer of specialty chemicals in Brazil; (2) Ultragaz, the leader in Brazil's liquefied petroleum gas (LPG) distribution market; and (3) Ultracargo, a leading provider of storage, transport, and handling services for chemicals and fuels.

Although the company sought inorganic growth, it had a demonstrated aversion to overpaying. Shortly after the IPO, for example, Ultrapar tried to acquire the petrochemical maker Copene, for which its IPO assets would have been essential. But before the deal could close, a large Brazilian construction firm offered a higher price, and CEO Paulo Cunha pulled out to avoid a bidding war. (Management later gave the money back to the shareholders through an extraordinary dividend.) Despite this and other aborted deals, Ultrapar was eager to pursue new avenues for growth.

Ipiranga was one of Brazil's largest conglomerates. It consisted of several separate companies in the fuel distribution business (CBPI and CPPI); the oil refining business (RIPI); and the petrochemical business (ICQ, IPQ, and a 29.5 percent share of Copesul, Brazil's second-largest petrochemicals producer). In 2006, Ipiranga had consolidated revenues of BRL 29 billion, EBITDA of BRL 1 billion,

(continued)

(continued)

and a net income of BRL 534 million. The company paid high dividends, but they frequently came at the expense of a high leverage ratio. And, for a variety of reasons, the company fuel-distribution profits had decreased for some time (the EBITDA margin was less than 2 percent in 2006).

Ipiranga had some synergies with Ultrapar's existing businesses. Its fuel distribution business shared some of the core competencies already dominated by Ultrapar. Moreover, the growing vehicle market in Brazil and the fragmentation of the market offered opportunities for obtaining additional scale and operational leverage through an acquisition.

On the one hand, failing to purchase Ipiranga might jeopardize Ultrapar's future growth. On the other hand, if the company overpaid, this would destroy shareholder value.

Complicating any deal was the fact that Ipiranga had a complex shareholding structure controlled by the members of just five families. By 2007, more than 60 different shareholders formed the controlling group, which had the majority of ON (voting) shares. They had a very strong shareholders' agreement which, for example, gave all of them veto rights on any major corporate reorganization or M&A deal. This agreement effectively locked these 60+ family members in, making it virtually impossible for a single family member to sell its shares. In addition, the five families shared control of the company through a myriad of subsidiaries.

Therefore, when Ultrapar helped lead a three-company consortium (which included Petrobras and Braskem) in the acquisition of Ipiranga in 2007, the deal involved a series of complex share-exchange transactions and a corporate restructuring that split Ipiranga's assets between the consortium partners:

- Ultrapar retained Ipiranga's fuel distribution business in the south and southeast of Brazil.
- Petrobras became the owner of the target's fuel business in the north, northeast, and mid-west regions.
- Petrobras and Braskem became the owners of Ipiranga's petrochemical arm, 40 percent and 60 percent, respectively.
- The refining assets were equally split between the three consortium partners.

Despite the complexity of the deal, its benefits were easy to recognize.

Following the acquisition, Ultrapar simplified Ipiranga's corporate structure, reduced costs, and better aligned the interests of managers and shareholders, allowing it to extract significant benefits. "We brought an amazing simplification to Ipiranga," said Cunha, Ultrapar CEO.

In the years after the deal, volumes increased 5–10 percent a year, and margins increased significantly. By 2010, Ipiranga's margins stood close to 3 percent, and EBITDA had improved to BRL 976 million from BRL 350 million in 2006. The acquisition also gave Ipiranga access to major investment opportunities with additional synergies. In 2008, for example, Ultrapar acquired Texaco's distribution business, including more than 2000 service stations in Brazil, which exposed Ipiranga to regions with higher growth in consumption. In addition, Ipiranga achieved substantial synergies (through better utilization of distribution terminals, improved efficiency, and greater economies of scale) in administrative functions, advertising, marketing, product, development, and so on, as well as gaining a truly nationwide fuel network.

Identify Hard *and* Soft Synergies

To think like a financial investor is to think *in detail* about what the synergies are, how they will be achieved, and who will be responsible for achieving them. And here is where many bidders fall down.

The biggest sources of value from most M&As are typically hard synergies that include the following:

Cost of Goods Sold When two entities merge there are often economies of scale, and the different functional strengths can be optimized. This allows the combined company to become more cost-efficient. There may also be potential cost savings related to purchasing activities, as the merged entity may be able to negotiate better conditions with suppliers. The 2007 merger of Delta Air Lines and Northwest Airlines is a prime example of a transaction motivated by a desire for greater cost synergies. The key driver for the deal was the anticipated savings of $500 million to be generated from more effective aircraft utilization, a more comprehensive route system, and from reduced overheads and operational efficiency.

SG&A There's usually a certain degree of overlap in administrative and selling expenses between the acquiring and target companies. For example, in the case of two publicly traded companies, the combined entity will require only a single investor relations department, one CEO, a combined HR department, and so on. Thus, it is reasonable to assume a reduction in selling, general, and administrative (SG&A) expenses for the target company in most M&As. The level of SG&A reduction depends on the degree of overlap (including geographical) between the companies. If the two firms are located in distinct regions, the potential for cost-cutting based on combined structures is often reduced. However, if the companies are located in the same region and sector, combining them can generate significant synergies.

The 1999 merger of Exxon and Mobil allowed the new company to achieve substantial synergies in this area. It was able to reduce costs by eliminating redundant operations and increase production and sales by combining complementary operations. (There were also technology synergies, as both companies owned proprietary technologies that could be used profitably in each other's oil and gas fields.)

CAPEX Merging companies may be able to reap Capital Expenditure (CAPEX) benefits. This is frequently the case with M&As in the pharmaceutical industry, where combining the R&D functions of two companies can produce significant CAPEX cost savings because of the overlapping portfolio of drugs under development. For example, when SmithKline Beecham was looking for target companies in 2000, it focused on R&D and revenue synergies. "[O]ur production costs, once we've developed a drug, are minimal … so when we looked at merging with Glaxo … we were talking about synergies in R&D," said CEO Jan Leschly in a May 2000 interview. "By merging the two organizations, we probably could save in the neighborhood of $500 million."

Sales Here, revenue synergies are related to possible cross-selling of products and services. Companies can obtain higher growth in new or existing markets. By leveraging each other's distribution networks or presenting a better and more complete product (and service) portfolio, the new entity might be able to increase its revenues relative to the two stand-alone companies. It is also possible to obtain revenue synergies owing to the greater pricing power achieved from reduced competition and higher market share. In 2010, ABB announced its acquisition of the U.S. electric motor manufacturer Baldor. Significant synergies were identified based on the potential for cross-selling through each other's distribution networks. In addition, the deal allowed Baldor to take advantage of ABB's global distribution and for better portfolios to be offered to customers, given that the two companies had complementary product lines.

Net Working Capital There can be better use of inventory, an impact on payment terms with suppliers, or different trade credit terms as a result of a merger. Before acquiring DF, you may recall, the FGB team identified several synergy opportunities related to supplier payment terms. Among other things, the two companies used a common credit card processor that was charging DF considerably more than FGB (because the latter was doing five times the amount of business with the supplier than DF). Contracts with that vendor—and other suppliers—could be addressed to negotiate better terms.

Taxes There are often financial gains to be explored related to tax optimization (for instance, goodwill amortization). Tax benefits can arise by taking advantage of tax laws and through better use of past net operating losses. If a profitable company acquires a company that has been accumulating losses, the acquiring company might be able to reduce its tax burden. In addition, a company can sometimes increase its amortization and depreciation charges after an acquisition, thereby savings taxes and increasing its value.

Although some companies do a fair job of identifying and calculating the value of "hard synergies," they frequently overlook "soft synergies." This is understandable, considering that most businesspeople are trained to think in terms of sales, revenues, costs, and taxes, rather than items that are difficult to quantify: talent, knowledge, agility, innovation, and so forth. Soft synergies can also produce higher revenues and lower costs. However, they are usually trickier to identify and achieve than hard synergies. Nevertheless, both hard and soft synergies should be plugged into financial models to ensure a proper valuation.

Jordi Costa, Vice President for Agribusiness, Sugar & Bioenergy at Bunge SA, noted that hard synergies are rarely missed because they are usually related to cost. "It is usually about cost, about amortizing FTEs. The same team with a few more resources can operate the new business and do a lot more. Then the previous team is not needed anymore. Those synergies are usually captured, but many times you don't buy a company just for that. You buy it more for the other capabilities they're going to bring. Usually, we calculate only the hard synergies, and the soft synergies are considered an upside potential."

In their financial models, most companies only consider and quantify the hard synergies, which means they never pay premiums based on softer synergies. In other words, while soft synergies are identified and presented to the board, they are not used to calculate the payment to the target company.

Calculate the Target's Stand-Alone Value and the Value with Synergies

The most common method of company valuation, free cash flow to the firm (FCFF), attempts to determine the enterprise value of the target by discounting all the cash flows over the life of the company. This lets the acquiring firm estimate the equity value by subtracting the debt value from the resulting enterprise value. In the FCFF method, it's usually assumed that a company has an infinite life. Thus, the analysis is performed in two parts: (1) an explicit forecast period and (2) a terminal value. The terminal value is estimated at the end of the forecast period and summarizes the present value of all future cash flows from that period onward.[10]

When valuing a company by FCFF in an M&A setting, the synergies are key determinants of the valuation. Importantly, company valuation by the discounted cash flow (DCF) method allows explicitly for the computation of the value of the synergies. Under the DCF model, it is common to consider two scenarios: stand-alone value and value with synergies.

The stand-alone valuation involves forecasting the cash flows that the target company is able to generate on its own. These base cash flows should not include any of the benefits that might result from the merger. Instead, cash flows for the target company must be forecast based on its business plan, a competitive analysis of the market, and the overall growth of the sector and the economy by performing the following steps:

1. Obtaining, for each year, the FCFF of the target company, according to current management plans, which should be consistent with industry trends and competitive positioning.
2. Discounting these cash flows at the weight average cost of capital (WACC) of the target company, which then provides the stand-alone enterprise value.
3. Obtaining the value of the equity of the company by subtracting the net debt value from the resulting enterprise value.[11]

The stand-alone value can be compared to the market value of the target if it's publicly traded, and may allow for an assessment of whether the target company is under- or overvalued in the market. Generally, the stand-alone value should not differ much from the current market value of the target (assuming it is publicly traded). In most situations, it is unlikely that the target is substantially under- or overvalued, and therefore, calibration of the stand-alone value allows the acquirer to understand some of the investors' perceptions of the target. Thus, the stand-alone valuation provides a floor in terms of the value that the bidder should pay in a negotiation. Rational shareholders of a target should never agree to sell their company for less than the stand-alone value.

Of course, the idea behind most M&As is that the synergies produced by the combined entities will generate higher cash flows following the merger. Therefore, when deciding whether to make an offer for a particular target, the acquirer needs to consider the possible sources of value and how much they are worth. Once all the projected synergies are incorporated into the cash flows, the acquirer obtains the *FCFF with synergies*. Then, by discounting the FCFF with synergies with the cost of capital, the buyer arrives at the full value of the target company, assuming all the anticipated synergies actually materialize.

Once the acquiring company calculates a stand-alone value of the target firm, as well as a value based on projected synergies, the proposed purchase price should fall somewhere between these two values so the target company's shareholders receive a premium.

In the real world, however, most bidders overpay relative to the value with synergies. More often than not, a huge premium is paid, and the value of those synergies is passed to the target's shareholders. That is why most deals destroy value. It's not that there are no synergies between the two companies. It's simply that the value of those synergies (which will accrue over many years) was paid upfront to the target's shareholders, leaving the acquirer's shareholders at a loss. (This is why the share price of the acquirer typically goes down following the announcement of a so-called bad deal.)

Arriving at reasonable numbers of the different synergy components requires rigorous analysis of both companies' operations and businesses. After the synergies have been identified, it is common to assume that they will be achieved gradually—normally in two or three years. In fact, the rule of thumb states that if the synergies have not been achieved within three years of the merger, they no longer exist. Therefore, once the merger is concluded, it is vital to base the post-integration plan on the synergies that were forecasted *before* the merger. Indeed, it is these synergies that define the price to be paid and, ultimately, the value creation of the merger. If they are not adequately pursued during the post-deal period, the M&A will not create value for the acquiring firm.

How Payment Methods Affect Deal Outcomes

Should target companies be purchased with cash, stock, or a mix of the two?

In most instances, the form of payment used in an M&A is heavily influenced by the interests of the target's shareholders and the financial constraints of the acquirer.

For the acquirer, a payment in cash must be financed with cash the company has on its balance sheet or through new issues of debt and/or equity. This, of course, raises issues related to financing and capital structure. For example, new issues of debt may negatively affect the company's credit rating—as it did with Telefónica (see the case study above). On the other hand, financial markets frequently interpret all-cash deals as a demonstration of the acquirer's confidence that the anticipated synergies will be achieved. For this reason, they are more likely to reward the acquirer's shareholders following the announcement of such a deal, rather than punishing them.

From the target's perspective, cash and stock deals can produce different tax exposures. For example, in a cash deal, the target's shareholders may have to immediately pay taxes based on their capital gains, whereas when stock is exchanged, the target stockholders can usually defer tax payments until they sell the shares.

Most important, cash and share payments have different risk implications. In a cash deal, the target shareholder receives a fixed amount, and does not incur any risk if expected synergies never materialize. On the other hand, by accepting payment in shares, the target shareholders effectively become shareholders of the new combined company. This means they will now have a stake in the future of the new company. If the synergies realized are greater than expected, the target shareholders will benefit from a likely increase in the new companies' stock price. If the combined entity fails to realize significant synergies, or the profitability of the new company takes a hit, these shareholders will suffer.

Paying with your own stock can be tempting, and cheaper, but it often proves to be a mistake for the acquirer. While it's true that, as shareholders of the newly combined company, the seller has more incentive to see that the merger is a success, paying with stock spreads the rewards, as well as the risks. By paying with cash, the acquiring company's managers and shareholders reap all of the rewards for themselves. According to Warren Buffett, one of his worst mistakes was to "issue 272,200 shares of Berkshire in buying [General Reinsurance in 1998], an act that increased our outstanding shares by a whopping 21.8%. My error caused Berkshire shareholders to give far more than they received (a practice that – despite the Biblical endorsement – is far from blessed when you are buying businesses)."[12]

Earnouts are another payment option to consider, though they are normally restricted to deals that involve the acquisition of small private companies. An earnout is essentially a contingency payment pegged to the future performance of the target—a legal document whose payment triggers are based on specific agreements for measuring progress. This enables the buyer to pay a fixed amount today and then, in the future, pay additional sums to the seller if certain performance metrics are achieved (usually over a two-year period).

Earnouts are especially useful when there are strong disagreements between the buyer and seller about future performance (and, thus, the estimated cash flows). Typically, the seller is more optimistic about its future performance than the buyer, which gives rise to substantial differences in valuations. If both parties agree on a higher valuation if certain performance goals are met, they can make that valuation differential contingent on meeting the targets. For the buyer, the earnout helps manage risk. Additional payments occur only if the business performs well or the synergies are realized. For the seller, the earnout can provide additional payments (relative to what a risk-averse buyer would pay) if the performance goals are met.

The chief problem with using earnouts derives from the post-acquisition integration and the complexity of defining performance goals. Once the deal has been completed, it sometimes becomes difficult to assess the performance of the target because it's now part of the buyer's combined operations. In addition, it's not unusual to encounter sellers with no interest in having contingency claims attached to the deal. Sometimes, the seller simply needs cash.

The most important question to ask before choosing a payment method is "What does the seller want, and why?" If the target is desperate for cash, there may be no room for discussion. But in many instances, the answer to this question can provide the buyer with bargaining leverage.

P&G's Purchase of Gillette: A Modified All-Stock Deal

Because of the negative tax and leverage consequences of all-cash M&A deals, acquiring companies often provide the target company's shareholders with shares of the acquiring company instead (or in addition). Of course, all-stock deals *also* have drawbacks—for example, the target's shareholders may not want the stock of the acquirer—so buyers sometimes develop hybrid offers that combine elements of both all-cash and all-stock transactions. Such was the case when Procter & Gamble (P&G) acquired Gillette in January 2005.

P&G created a modified all-stock offer that consisted of the following:

- P&G would issue 0.975 shares of its stock for each share of Gillette. This would allow Gillette's shareholders to avoid the immediate payment of capital-gains taxes while helping P&G retain more cash.
- In addition, P&G also agreed to repurchase $18–$22 billion of P&G stock over an 18-month period—a component of the deal designed to further appeal to Gillette shareholders. The move would provide them with a completely tax-free transaction that allowed them to own (if they so wished) shares of the combined company or (if they didn't wish) to sell the stock back to P&G for cash.
- The share buyback would also result in reduced shareholder dilution. By the end of the 18-month repurchase timeframe, the transaction would comprise about 60 percent stock and 40 percent cash.

There was a risk, though, that the buyback program would negatively affect P&G's credit rating with the major rating agencies. Shortly after the deal was announced, for example, Standard & Poor's, Moody's, and Fitch Ratings informed P&G that the borrowing that it would undertake to finance the stock repurchase had triggered a reexamination of its credit rating, which might subsequently be downgraded. Fortunately, by the time P&G began issuing debt in August 2005 to complete the buyback, it still enjoyed strong ratings from Moody's and Standard & Poor's (Aa3 and AA-, respectively).

Like other mergers and acquisitions, especially those involving a highly prized target, the P&G offer included a break-up fee to protect the acquiring company. In the event Gillette solicited a higher price from another buyer, the new acquirer would be obliged to pay P&G $1.9 billion, which amounted to more than 3 percent of the deal's total value.

Although the two consumer-products giants agreed to the break-up fee, they did not employ a "collar" on the value of the shares that P&G offered—a potentially risky move. Common in many M&A transactions, a collar creates a ceiling and a floor on the value of the shares offered to complete the deal. By establishing a price range, the collar assures the shareholders of both companies that they will be protected from any fluctuations in the price of the acquirer's stock while the transaction awaits shareholder approval—a process that typically ranges from three to six months.

Although the lack of a collar surprised many observers, it did not generate any controversy. What *did* generate headline-grabbing notoriety was the $164 million in compensation that Gillette CEO James Kilts received from the merger, the combined $90 million in fees earned by the three investment banks involved in the deal, and the fears of Gillette's workforce that many jobs would be eliminated—fears that later proved to be exaggerated.[13]

Measures to Prevent Overpaying

It should be clear by now that the biggest mistake that a buyer can make is overpaying. When the acquiring company pays too high a premium, the deal will destroy value even if every anticipated synergy is achieved ahead of schedule. Perhaps the most common cause of overpayment is irrational attachment to the deal by enthusiastic CEOs who convince themselves that the target must be purchased at almost any price.

Rather than championing costly deals, the internal M&A team, CEO, and the board of directors must strive to be the voice of reason. They *should* challenge assumptions and continually question the numbers, including numbers that have been deliberately set too low by synergy "owners" who under-promise so they can later over-deliver (also known as "sandbagging"). Unfortunately, "should challenge" does not always translate into "will challenge," thanks to the well-documented tendency of many CEOs and boards to overvalue evidence that supports their pre-existing views while discounting any evidence to the contrary ("confirmation bias"). Confirmation bias is particularly common among managers with a track record of M&A success, causing them to believe that their instinct and judgment are infallible. This overconfidence can lead them to make ill-advised acquisitions.

In theory, an internal M&A team composed of cross-functional managers—including people from finance, operations, marketing, sales, and HR—should serve as an effective check on confirmation biases, impulsiveness, and even hubris. In practice, however, charismatic and powerful CEOs have a habit of persuading skeptics to their point of view and/or steamrolling the M&A team to the sidelines.

Therefore, I advise acquiring companies to establish a rival, independent team (preferably an external one) that can supplement the analysis and recommendations of the first team. This group should serve as Devil's Advocate, providing invaluable checks and balances. This will help ensure that people who oppose the deal (internal and external) will have the courage to speak up, reducing the likelihood that "group think" will carry the day.

Another alternative, used by some companies, is to use internal "think tanks" composed in part of retired managers, to serve as a check on the M&A team. These think tanks are specifically charged with challenging deals, but they typically ask the right questions to make sure the thinking is solid. And they basically test certain metrics and parameters to make sure the people really thought through the details in developing the forecast. They challenge growth plans, synergy plans, cost assumptions—anything that goes into the income statement forecast.

Solar A/S group's Jeppesen agreed that it's crucial to check the tendency toward group think during M&As, citing what he dubbed the "Tenth Man Rule."

> I once saw a movie called World War Z. While describing his agency's approach to intelligence gathering, one character talks about 'the Tenth Man' – meaning that if nine people agree on a course of action, a tenth man is bound to prove them wrong. So it's important to find someone who will take the opposite point of view – someone who will focus only on the things that could go wrong. And if you follow the Tenth Man Rule, you have to do it in a systematic way because what happens at companies is there's a tendency for the majority to simply bull-dozer the internal opposition. And I think these people have to come from the outside so they aren't risking their necks.

In addition to employing a Tenth Man, acquisition companies should identify and codify "kill switches"—scenarios that will automatically trigger termination of the deal—during the "pre-mortem" analysis. In lieu of this (or in addition), Aperam's Jalan recommends a very strong SWOT analysis. "We try to anticipate as much as we can in terms of what could be the main pitfalls in that industry and market or challenges to the company's footprint, and how these could be addressed. These are addressed in SWOT."

Every member of the independent deal team should clearly understand, and be fluent in key financial terms, including a mindset of value creation. A deep understanding of value drivers is also needed. Otherwise, team members are less likely to contribute their best efforts—the kind of bottom-up inputs that will ensure that the final valuation is reasonable instead of overly generous.

Synergy Summits

Most acquirers focus on capturing traditional sources of value close to their existing lines of business. Hence, the "traditional" approach to integration is to employ templates, checklists, and rigorous process management to zero in on the cost savings associated with reducing redundant operations and people, while avoiding risk. Using this approach, new sources of synergy and value are often overlooked, which may explain (in part) the high M&A failure rate.

I recommend that, post-closing, companies undertake a comprehensive review and revision of all the synergies via synergy summits/workshops. Here, cross-functional teams should look for ways to meet the synergy targets and then develop realistic plans for achieving them. The teams begin by creating initial plans for reaching the targets, analyzing the data to determine if these plans will work, and then debating various options for extracting even greater value. To ensure greater accountability, this also is an ideal time to nominate key "synergy owners."

The groups' focus should be on hatching new ideas and identifying challenges, not simply attaching revised numbers to the synergies. After the brainstorming phase is complete, the group should review the ideas and select those they wish to pursue. The finalized synergy goals should be incorporated into the financial plan as soon as possible and a rewards system created for the synergy owners.

Thanks (in part) to this level of collaboration between companies, noted Huibert Vigeveno, Shell was able to quickly increase its synergy-value estimates (and advanced the synergy-capture deadlines) from the purchase of BG from $2.5 billion to $4.5 billion. "Because we put people together from BG and Shell, working along the same areas of activities … we really co-created something. We got an ecosystem going … creating this atmosphere of trust, collaboration and clarity of what needs to be done." The two companies created a team spirit of people working together well before the acquisition was complete.

By the end of many summits, synergy targets are frequently reset to higher levels and the participants have become even more committed to the strategy. By engaging the appropriate managers in shaping new targets and plans, and by giving them greater ownership, synergy summits encourage participants to ruthlessly focus on the big value drivers and diligently track them during the integration.

Summary

When deals are announced, financial markets do an uncanny job of predicting the long-term consequences. In most cases, the markets punish shareholders of the acquirer and reward shareholders of the target. For this reason, M&A teams are advised to think like a financial investor. Employ financial models to determine if deals are worth pursuing, exercise the discipline to say "no" when the numbers don't add up, avoid bidding wars, and never fall in love with deals. Emotions, overconfidence, and ego are leading causes of value destruction in M&As.

It is critical to identify what the synergies are, how they will be achieved, and who will be responsible for achieving them, including both "hard" and "soft" synergies. Hard synergies are easier to quantify, and usually relate to costs and taxes. Soft synergies are normally related to talent, mindset, and expertise, and are more difficult to achieve. I recommend that synergies be revised, post-close, in synergy summits/workshops that involve appropriate managers from different functions, and that focus on both hard and soft synergies. Team members should ruthlessly track the key value drivers.

Prior to the closing, the acquiring company should calculate a stand-alone value of the target firm as it currently exists *and* a value based on the projected synergies. The proposed purchase price should fall somewhere between these two values so the target company's shareholders also receive a premium. Unfortunately, most bidders overpay relative to the value with synergies. This is why most deals destroy value. To avoid this, acquiring companies should ask, "How much is this deal worth to us," and then offer less. And both bidders and sellers should evaluate how different methods of payment are likely to affect the deal's outcome.

To prevent overpaying, it's advisable to establish an independent team (preferably external) tasked with challenging the deal. This can prevent "group think," helping to ensure that those who oppose the deal will speak up and serve as a counter to CEO confirmation bias. They should also work to prevent sandbagging—deliberate underestimation of the synergies—and develop kill switches that will trigger termination of the deal if certain thresholds are crossed.

Questions for Future M&As

- Does your company assign the synergies (hard and soft) to particular members of the deal team?
- Do you utilize financial models to determine if M&As are worth the effort?
- During the analysis phase, do you develop "kill switches" that will trigger termination of the deal under certain circumstances?
- Has your company ever walked away from a deal?
- Does your company verify, ex-post, valuations done for prior deals, as well as the validity of the forecasts used then? And does it have the learning systems in place, to assure that past mistakes will not be repeated?
- Have you ever entered into a deal—or failed to walk away—for emotional reasons?
- Do you appoint independent teams (internal or external) to challenge assumptions and/or entire deals?
- Have you organized and/or participated in a synergy workshop or a similar forum?
- Does your firm maintain an updated list of *external* advisers—law firms, investment banks, auditors, and so on—so you can move quickly when an M&A opportunity arises?

Notes

1. See Andrade G., M. Mitchell, and E. Stafford, 2001, New Evidence and Perspectives on Mergers, *Journal of Economic Perspectives*; and Betton, S., B.E. Eckbo, and K.S. Thorburn, 2008, "Corporate Takeovers" in B.E. Eckbo (ed.) *Handbook of Corporate Finance: Empirical Corporate Finance*, Vol. 2, Elsevier/North-Holland.

2. Tim Loughran and Anand M Vijh, "Do Long-Term Shareholders Benefit from Corporate Acquisitions?" *Journal of Finance*, 1997.

3. http://aswathdamodaran.blogspot.com/2012/12/acquisition-archives-winners-and-losers.html

4. Warren Buffet, "Here's the metric I use when investing in banks." *CNBC*, February 27, 2017.

5. For analyses of the different determinants of merger returns, see (among others) Asquith, P., R.F. Bruner, and D.W. Mullins, Jr., 1983, "The Gains to Bidding Firms from Mergers." *Journal of Financial Economics*; Morck, R., A. Shleifer, and R.W. Vishny, 1990, "Do Managerial Objectives Drive Bad Acquisitions?" *Journal of Finance*; Lang, L., Stulz, R., and Walkling, R.A., "A test of the free cash flow hypothesis: The case of bidder returns." *Journal of Financial Economics*, 1991; Maloney, M.T., R.E. McCormick, and M.L. Mitchell, 1993, "Managerial Decision Making and Capital Structure." *Journal of Business*; G. WILLIAM SCHWERT, "Hostility in Takeovers: In the Eyes of the Beholder?" *The Journal of Finance*, 2000; Gayle L. DeLong, "Stockholder gains from focusing versus diversifying bank mergers." *Journal of Financial Economics*, 2001; Andrade G., M. Mitchell, and E. Stafford, 2001, "New Evidence and Perspectives on Mergers." *Journal of Economic Perspectives*; Moeller, S.B., F.P. Schlingemann, and R.M. Stulz, 2004, "Firm Size and the Gains from Acquisitions." *Journal of Financial Economics*; Moeller, S., F. Schlingemann, and R. Stulz, 2005, "Wealth Destruction on a Massive Scale? A Study of Acquiring Firms in the Recent Merger Wave." *Journal of Finance*; and Dos Santos, M.B., V. Errunza, and D. Miller, 2008, "Does Corporate International Diversification Destroy Value? Evidence from Cross-Border Mergers and Acquisitions." *Journal of Banking and Finance*; Martynova M., and L. Renneboog, 2011, "The Performance of the European Market for Corporate Control: Evidence from the Fifth Takeover Wave." *European Financial Management*; Ahern K., D. Daminelli, and C. Fracassi, 2013, "Lost in Translation? The Effect of Cultural Values on Mergers around the World." *Journal of Financial Economics*.

6. James Heskett, "Should We Brace Ourselves for Another Era of M&A Value Destruction?" Harvard Business School, April 5, 2004.

7. Morningstar Equity Research, February 2010.

8. Andrew Pollack and Michael J. de la Merce, "Monsanto Abandons $47 Billion Takeover Bid for Syngenta." *The New York Times*, August 26, 2015.

9. Matthew Campbell, Andrew Noël and Ed Hammond, "Syngenta Rejects $45 Billion Takeover Offer from Monsanto." *Bloomberg*, May 8, 2015.
10. Fernandes, Nuno, "Finance for Executives: A Practical Guide for Managers." NPV Publishing, 2014, pg. 50.
11. Ibid, pg. 51.
12. https://www.gobankingrates.com/personal-finance/7-investing-mistakes-warren-buffett-regrets/
13. David P. Stowell, "Teaching Note: Procter & Gamble's Acquisition of Gillette." Kellogg School of Management, Northwestern University, 2007.

5

Move Fast and Communicate Transparently

While the long-term goal of M&As is to increase profits through synergy capture, most M&As also generate a dangerous, short-term side effect: *uncertainty*. And in the business world, uncertainty is nobody's ally. When left unchecked, this state of mind gives rise to anxiety, which can then result in a mass exodus of the companies' customers and most talented employees.

Numerous studies have confirmed that employees (especially of the target company) often experience fear and anxiety about a wide range of issues once they learn that a deal has been initiated, including fears related to their job security and status, their career trajectories, and even their personal identities.

Whether employee anxiety is triggered by a formal announcement or baseless rumors, it can translate into low morale and low productivity as distracted workers spend more time worrying about their careers—or searching for new jobs—than on day-to-day tasks. In turn, this loss of focus and morale may contribute to higher-than-normal rates of customer attrition as employees pay too little attention to clients or seek to actively poach them.

Higher Attrition Rates Can Last for Years

Research on rates of employee attrition following M&As reveals that roughly one-quarter of executives in an acquired company's top management team will leave within the first year. This is about triple the departure rate at comparable companies that have not been purchased. Moreover, an additional 15 percent of the target firm's managers will leave in the second year. Once upon

© The Author(s) 2019
N. Fernandes, *The Value Killers*, https://doi.org/10.1007/978-3-030-12216-4_5

a time, it was widely assumed that executive turnover returned to normal after Year 2, but according to research by Jeffrey A. Krug, the studies on which this assumption was based failed to examine the turnover of the executives who were hired to *replace* the original managers. As it turns out, executives who join the organization after the merger *also* leave at higher-than-normal attrition rates, beginning about two years after the acquisition. In fact, these new hires quit the company at double the normal rate for at least nine years following the M&A.[1]

Krug expresses little surprise at the departure rates of the original executives, many of whom leave involuntarily or because of reduced status or low morale, and he speculates that many of the new hires leave because they are inadvertently "set up to fail." Acquiring firms frequently restructure and downsize the target shortly after the deal. At the same time, senior management often expects the reduced workforce to maintain (or increase) productivity. For this and other reasons, the performance of many acquired companies doesn't improve very much, and it's the new executives who often shoulder the blame.

On the customer side, attrition can be just as high—if not higher. A survey conducted by The Deloitte Center for Banking Solutions of bank customers who recently underwent an M&A transition discovered that *48 percent* of the newly acquired customers had already switched banks or were likely to switch banks in the near future. According to the poll, 36 percent of these disgruntled customers abandoned the target bank for emotional reasons—usually because they feared change or felt undervalued by the acquiring company.[2]

Speed and Effective Communication Are Imperative

Speed and timely, transparent communication are essential during and after an M&A transaction. A prolonged bidding and negotiating period increases the risk that the best employees will leave, information will be leaked, and competitors will pre-empt the deal or steal value from the soon-to-be combined entity. To prevent these outcomes, it is vital to address integration challenges early in the M&A process. Hence, updates of headquarters, clear KPIs, and action plans for the integration are fundamental. "Speed is critical" said Casper Kirketerp-Moeller of Clever A/S. "If you don't have a good [integration] plan before Day One – value is destroyed immediately. If you start off on the wrong foot, you will start to build momentum from the wrong foot …

so during preparation, it's important to understand the nuts and bolts of the target and get the target's management engaged at a hands-on level. They cannot do this from a board room."

Halbart Völker of NIBC Bank agreed, adding: "There's a huge benefit in using the momentum that follows the announcement of the deal. Then you have a period where you can actually make changes quite rapidly. If you wait too long, things become more and more complicated. Speed is quite important."

As a rule, companies that move quickly and engage in transparent communication during M&As are better at retaining focus and reducing uncertainty among their key stakeholders. A common—and very big—mistake made by many buyers is to postpone the dissemination of important information until the details have been finalized. From the perspective of the acquirer, this may seem logical. Among employees and customers, however, such delays may just exacerbate their existing anxieties, particularly when there's nothing to fill the "communication void" but rumors and speculation.

For Employees, Bad News Is Often Better Than No News

It's natural for employees and clients to seek out information from both formal and informal sources to help alleviate the uncertainty surrounding M&As. Employees want to know whether they will have a job tomorrow, while suppliers and customers want to know if and when the new organization will introduce new policies, products, and pricing. Because uncertainty frequently leads to dissatisfaction, anger, and a desire to leave, communicating *any* news is often better than leaving important constituencies in the dark—even when that news may not be welcome. For example, if worker layoffs and plant closings are likely to occur, do not wait until the final decisions are made to discuss the topic. Be honest and upfront with the impacted audiences even if you're not yet sure how many workers will be fired and which plants will be shuttered.

Of course, when it comes to preventing an exodus of your best employees and customers, *how* you communicate such messages can be just as important—if not more important—than the actual content of the messages. And if one of your goals is to quash negative rumors instead of feeding them, good timing is also critical.

For example, during an acquisition by NIBC Bank, the company's spokespeople met with a variety of audiences to discuss the company's plans, including the need to lay off roughly 10–15 percent of the target's workforce. Instead of withholding that information until management knew *precisely* when the layoffs would occur and which employees would be affected, the spokespeople delivered carefully crafted messages that emphasized the unfortunate, but logical, necessity for this downsizing. According to Halbart Völker, speaking about a successful deal in a company where he was the CFO, the message was "supported by clear financial evidence that there was actually no way around it. We showed them individual P&L statements of the different businesses to make it very clear that certain business lines were heavy loss-makers, and that this was personnel-related. There were too many full-time employees on the payroll without enough revenue to support them. So we didn't just deliver the message that 'this doesn't work.' We presented the information in combination with our plans to make fair arrangements for the people who would be laid off."

Meet with New Customers ASAP

During the deal phase and immediately after the closing, acquiring companies sometimes take customers for granted—both existing customers and those they acquire from the target company. With so many managers focused on getting the deal done and combining the operations of the two organizations, clients can easily get lost in the shuffle. It's no wonder, then, that savvy competitors often decide to strike during the deals, viewing these periods as prime opportunities for scooping up customers who feel ignored or underappreciated.

Although it's important for the acquirer to maintain adequate focus on its current customers, it's especially critical to communicate with the *target's* customers—as quickly as possible and in personalized ways. The executives with whom I spoke indicated that while sending emails and making calls to new customers are a good start, face-to-face meetings should also be arranged within weeks—if not days. As soon as possible, assure these new customers that, despite the change in ownership, they are a top priority.

After an acquisition by Bunge SA, for example, the company's commercial team scheduled in-person meetings with 20 of its new customers within just 15 days. "You have to move fast," noted Jordi Costa. "Some of your synergies may depend on these customers, so you don't want to lose them to competitors – and you don't want to lose their contact information. If an employee of the target thinks he's going to be fired, he may try to get the customer to leave with him. Or he may take the contact information, and suddenly that information disappears from the system."

From the customer's point of view, he said, the worst thing that can happen is that he's sitting there, "knowing he's been bought and thinking, 'nobody is sending me a new sales representative. They didn't call me; they didn't visit me.' We always try to establish personal contact with the customer to explain the new company, and we do it systematically."

Although, Bunge SA typically retains the target's sales team and immediately arranges for personal visits or sends letters (when there was no prior personal connection/contact), Costa stressed that the target's customers are usually customers of the *company*, not individual salespeople. "Personal links matter, but ultimately, the financing and other services are provided by companies, not individuals."

Unfortunately, communicating with the target's employees and customers during the deal phase is often hampered by the confidentiality requirements imposed by anti-trust regulators. More than one executive I interviewed complained that, during this period, it's common for rumors to fly and for managers of the acquirer to receive phone calls from customers and suppliers who know that a deal is imminent and want to learn the details.

There is little that the parties to an M&A can legally communicate during this phase, because they are usually prohibited from contacting would-be customers until the transaction is cleared by the appropriate regulatory agencies. What they *can* do, however, is start planning (and refining their plans) for what will happen the day the deal is announced. What's more, as soon as possible, the buyer should involve the target's management in the integration planning. This was what Royal Dutch Shell did before it merged with BG Group plc in February 2016.

The Shell-BG Merger: A Master Class in Communication

To achieve one of the most successful and seamless mergers in recent history, Shell's integration planning began as soon as the deal was announced in April 2015 to ensure that the combined company would capture all the anticipated synergies and retain the best talent.

To this end, management teams from both companies immediately began working together at a neutral location. "We could not have achieved what we did if we had worked separately during this planning phase, although we were very conscious, of course, that before antitrust approvals were obtained, we needed to ensure that we operated our businesses entirely independently," said transition CEO Huibert Vigeveno. "We also paid a lot of attention to how we would retain the best talent in the combined group. Rather than be driven by a preference for employees within any one of the companies, the priority was always about doing what's right for the newly combined organization in a way that was equally fair, respectful, and transparent to all employees."[3]

(continued)

(continued)

As it turned out, the talent retention and joint planning efforts were mutually reinforcing. Thanks to the successful collaboration between the Shell and BG management teams to produce a smooth integration, it was easier for Shell to recruit BG executives for new positions in the combined company. To further facilitate this process, Shell hosted a workshop (before the merger announcement) at which managers from BG were interviewed for new jobs.

Of equal importance to the successful integration was the massive communications initiative that the combined organization launched on Day One. Beginning February 15, senior leaders from both organizations visited key locations across the globe to discuss the new company's plans, address major concerns, and answer questions.

During my interview with Vigeveno, he described his experiences talking with the employees. In the very first (Day One) town hall meeting with employees of BG's headquarters at Thames Valley Park, U.K., "I said, 'I'll treat you with openness and respect,'" said Vigeveno. "I understand that there are three questions on your minds. One is, Will I have a job, and when will I know? The second is, Will you close down Thames Valley Park. The third is, Will you force me into a job at Shell that I don't want?"

"'Will I have a job, and when will I know?' I said 'I don't know yet because I don't know you. This is the first day that we really can start to get to know you. We have a whole program in place to get to know you over the first 45 days. And from that, we will start working towards the target operating model.'"

"On the second question, 'Will you close down Thames Valley Park and when?' I told them that we would have in-depth review about real estate, but at the moment, I could not tell them what the outcome would be. But as it was such a significant factor for them, I would come back to them in person to tell them where the review was and what outcome it would have."

"On the third point, 'Will you force me a job into Shell which I don't want,' I told them, 'No, I will not force you into a job in Shell you do not want.'"

"In a town hall later in April, when we *did* know the outcome of the real estate, I was quite open. I said, 'I can now tell you that it is our intention to close Thames Valley Park by the end of this year.' And then I outlined the reasons for making that decision. And I told them in person – not via email, not via video. *In person.* I've made many speeches in my life, but I've never had it so quiet. But I think people appreciated that at least they knew where they stood. What I often find is, the only thing worse than negative news is not knowing. It's the uncertainty that's most difficult for people, so if you can create certainty, I think you always should."

This example, of how Vigeveno framed his messages for every audience, along with the strategies and tactics employed, provides an excellent model of how to communicate with major stakeholders after an M&A.

Use Your Time Wisely

A lot can be done before the actual close, so use the time wisely.

As the Shell-BG merger illustrates, preparation is a key factor that enables companies to move fast during the deal period—preparation of the communication plans, the commercial plans, systems, cultural integration, and so on. The period prior to the closing is also ideal for identifying and modeling the synergies via "synergy workshops" (see Chap. 4 for details). At these summits, managers from both companies should assemble to try to achieve even greater synergies than originally anticipated, with the original synergy estimates serving as a baseline. By adopting such an approach, Shell increased its synergies from $2.5 billion to $3.5 billion and then to $4 billion.

Again, it's also important for management to maintain a focus on customers and actual business operations during this period.

Summary

Speed is essential during and after a transaction. A prolonged bidding and negotiating period increases the risk that the best employees will leave, information will be leaked, and competitors will pre-empt the deal or steal value from the soon-to-be combined entity.

Uncertainty and lack of communication often lead to a talent exodus. Research on the rates of employee attrition following M&As reveals that roughly one-quarter of executives in an acquired company's top management team leave within the first year, with another 15 percent leaving in the second year. Often, these are the organization's most talented people.

Don't wait to communicate until every major detail of the integration is finalized. For example, if closing the target's headquarters is decided, it is usually better to communicate the bad news to the stakeholders than to withhold it. Where communication is lacking, rumors and speculation are likely to fill the void.

It's also important for management to maintain a focus on actual business operations, during the merger period. During the deal phase, many companies take customers for granted, and competitors may use this period to scoop them up. When it comes to newly acquired customers, be sure to communicate as quickly as possible, and preferably in person. Above all, it's vital to assure new customers that, despite the change in ownership, they are a top priority.

Address integration challenges early in the process. Updates of headquarters, clear KPIs, and action plans for the integration are fundamental. Of course, during the negotiation period, only a few individuals are involved, and no open communication can exist between the two organizations. Notwithstanding this challenge, it's important to involve the target's management as soon as possible. While waiting for anti-trust and other regulators, plan for Day One. Royal Dutch Shell and BG used this period to involve management teams from both companies in the integration planning—a joint effort that produced one of the most successful and seamless mergers in recent history.

Preparation is the key factor that enables companies to move fast. Preparation of communication plans, commercial plans, systems, and cultural integration can be undertaken, as can "synergy workshops."

Companies that move quickly and engage in clear and transparent communication during deals are better at retaining focus and reducing uncertainty among their key stakeholders.

Questions for Future M&As

- Does your company execute an M&A and communicate it to all stakeholders as fast as possible?
- What was the average attrition rate among your targets' employees—voluntary and involuntary—in the two years after previous deals?
- Do you communicate fast and clearly with customers during an M&A?
- What communication strategies and tactics have you used to reduce uncertainty and anxiety among employees?
- What messages does your company use to help quell such fears and anxiety?
- How quickly does your company engage with soon-to-be-acquired customers, and what communication methods are used?
- In what ways do you involve the target's management in the integration process?

Notes

1. Jeffrey A. Klug, "Why Do They Keep Leaving?" *Harvard Business Review*, February 2003.
2. Casey Boggs, "Poor Communication after a Merger Drives Customers Away." *American Banker*, February 14, 2013.
3. "Delivering a world-class integration in oil and gas." McKinsey & Company, February 2017.

6

Conclusion: Closing the Deal, But at What Price?

If there is one overriding "take-away" from this book, it is this: If the acquiring company pays too much for the target, it will destroy value, even if all of the projected synergies materialize. This seems both simple and obvious, but the reality is that most companies overpay. In fact, one could make an argument that, directly or indirectly, overpayment is *the cause* of the high M&A failure rate. It is the direct cause when a buyer overvalues the target's assets or overestimates anticipated synergies—as was the case when HP purchased Autonomy (see Chap. 1). It is an indirect cause when other factors (e.g., the culture clash that ensued after the Daimler-Benz/Chrysler merger) cause millions or billions of dollars in predicted synergies to later evaporate (see Chap. 3).

As we have seen, it *is* possible to beat the long odds against M&A success, but this requires rigorous planning and attention to detail, starting in the pre-acquisition phase. It also requires a thorough understanding and meticulous execution of the Five Golden Rules. Before closing this book, let's summarize the rules again, along with the key messages.

The Five Golden Rules: Key Messages

1: Don't Rely on Investment Bankers for Valuation In a financial and advisory capacity, investment banks can play an important role, but they should not be relied upon to provide the final valuation or negotiate the sale. This is because investment banks typically receive success fees for closing deals,

© The Author(s) 2019
N. Fernandes, *The Value Killers*, https://doi.org/10.1007/978-3-030-12216-4_6

regardless of whether the transactions create value for the shareholders. In short, investment banks have an incentive to *always* favor the deal, even when it doesn't serve the client's best interests.

Because companies shouldn't rely solely on outside advice for valuations, they must have (or develop) strong in-house valuation skills, from the top executives down. Otherwise, they are more likely to overpay. Vodafone's $180 billion acquisition of Mannesmann in 2000 is a notorious example (see Chap. 2). The deal erased tens of billions of dollars, largely because the investment bankers developed a flawed valuation.

Whenever possible, companies should develop valuations in-house or with the aid of third-party advisers who are less likely to be biased. Therefore, all employees who are involved in providing estimates should understand the principles of M&A value creation, as well as basic valuation skills. The key principles of valuation include the stand-alone value of the target company; its value with synergies; cash-flows and their changes due to the deal; current market capitalization; market multiples; transaction multiples; and previous premiums paid.

2: Avoid "Strategic" Deals There are many good, quantifiable reasons for doing M&A deals. They include increasing a company's product range, broadening its distribution, improving its manufacturing capabilities, and reducing unit costs. Unfortunately, there are just as many bad reasons. They include boosting the CEO's ego and salary, empire-building, and doing a "strategic deal"—a catchall phrase for a transaction whose benefits cannot be quantified. When the CEO says, "This is a strategic deal. We'd be foolish not to do it," the opposite is almost always true. The disastrous $165 billion merger between AOL and Time Warner in 2000 is the quintessential example. That deal had no financial justification, but was nevertheless labeled "strategic."

Boards of directors can, and should, play a critical role in preventing bad deals. They can do this by restraining CEO overconfidence and insisting that discussions focus on the facts of value creation. "Why an M&A? Why this company, and why now?" These are the crucial questions to which a board must demand answers.

To serve as a check on dubious deals, however, directors need to possess both the skills and independence. Where knowledge and expertise are lacking, they should hire independent advisers to assist with valuing the target and identifying the biggest risks. It is key that every synergy be clearly identified and quantified and that the acquirer know when, how, and who is going to achieve them.

3: Link the Before and After Companies must build a continuous process that links the pre-deal phase, the transaction phase, and the post-merger period. To accomplish this, senior executives should be involved from the start.

Historically, companies that destroy value in M&As deploy different teams during and after the deal, and they fail to properly manage the post-integration merger. In the best of all possible worlds, companies will assign the same team members to every phase of the transaction. If this isn't possible, it is critical that the "owners of the synergies" be involved *before*, as well as after, the deal is closed.

The initial due diligence is crucial because it provides the rationale for the valuation and deal structure. It allows companies to see how the merged organization can increase revenues or reduce costs, what the main risk factors are, and what roles the newly combined management teams will play. Before their 2008 merger, InBev and Anheuser-Busch determined which managers would comprise the joint team and how that team would then manage the combined entity (see Chap. 2).

Drafting heretofore uninvolved managers to lead the new organization or business units is a frequent mistake and one that eliminates accountability. If a manager is charged with achieving specific synergies, that manager should be incentivized to achieve those targets and avoid failure. This means that estimates during pre-deal phase must be thoroughly followed through in the post-merger phase. If pre-deal estimates are used to justify a valuation, then, in the post-merger period, those numbers must materialize for the deal to create value. And someone must be held accountable for the pre-deal forecasts.

Although some executives scapegoat "culture" to mask their own failures, the importance of cultural alignment should not be underrated. When cultural considerations are absent from planning, many problems can ensue, including diminished employee productivity and high attrition rates.

Should culture ever be a deal killer? Yes, but potential culture clashes can be identified before there's even a deal to be "killed." At well-run companies, "culture landmines" are identified—and potential remedies discussed—well before the deal closes. Many solutions are available. The "right" solutions depend on the M&A's purpose and its sources of value.

4: Think Like a Financial Investor Companies must be willing to cancel any M&A deal that goes above the "walk-away price." They should not get involved in auctions, and they should *never* fall in love with deals. This means that CEOs must either control their emotions or the board must control those emotions for them. Overconfidence is a notorious value killer.

The acquiring company should create a stand-alone value of the target firm as it is now and also develop a value with all the projected synergies included. The purchase price should be somewhere between these two valuations. Because most bidders overpay relative to the value with synergies, companies must ask, "How much is this deal really worth to us?" and then offer less.

It is critical to identify what the synergies are, how they will be achieved, and who will achieve them—both "hard" and "soft" synergies. I recommend that synergies be revised, post-closing, in synergy workshops that include the appropriate managers from different functions.

To prevent overpaying, acquirers can also establish an independent team whose job is *challenging* the deal. This can prevent "group think" by ensuring that people who oppose the deal have a "license" to speak their minds. The team should also prevent sand-bagging—the deliberate underestimation of the synergies—and establish kill switches that will trigger cancelation of the deal if certain circumstances arise.

5: Move Fast and Communicate Transparently Companies that communicate quickly and continuously during deals do a better job of retaining their focus and reducing uncertainty among customers and employees. Talent exodus is a real risk in most M&As, so senior managers must be ready to answer the "What happens to me?" questions when employees ask them.

Speed is also crucial during and after the transaction. An overly long bidding and negotiating period creates additional risks—risks of information leaks, employee exits, and competitors preempting the deal. And if synergies are not been achieved within two or three years after closing, it's because they have either evaporated or never really existed.

Don't wait to communicate until the integration details are set in stone. It's usually better to communicate something—even bad news—to the key stakeholders than to allow rumors and speculation to grab hold of their imaginations (and then their behaviors).

Address the integration challenges early and often and involve the target's management in this process as soon as possible. Even as you wait for government regulators to give the "green light," start planning for Day One. This is what Royal Dutch Shell and BG did to help produce one of the most successful and seamless mergers in recent history (see Chap. 5).

Finally, management must not become so distracted during the deal that its focus is entirely pulled away from the firm's day-to-day operations, including adequate communication with customers and other business partners.

* * *

If most or all of the Five Golden Rules are ignored, there is little that a merged company can do to compensate for the mistakes. Prevention is always the best remedy.

Successful acquirers develop models to identify the pros and cons of a deal, they avoid bidding wars, they exercise the discipline to walk away from bad deals, and they establish processes to keep CEO emotions in check.

It is not enough to have an internal M&A department (or business development group). Most companies have these, but still fail. Instead, successful M&As require that business and finance work together. It requires that business executives be aware of how M&As can create value, as well as their role in that value-creation process.

If more companies follow the Five Golden Rules, the years ahead will feature a much higher quality of M&As, and not just higher quantities.

List of Case Studies/Companies

© The Author(s) 2019
N. Fernandes, *The Value Killers*, https://doi.org/10.1007/978-3-030-12216-4

Index[1]

---

[1]Note: Page numbers followed by 'n' refer notes.

© The Author(s) 2019
N. Fernandes, *The Value Killers*, https://doi.org/10.1007/978-3-030-12216-4

Printed by Printforce, the Netherlands